Comptroller of the Currency
Administrator of National Banks

Interest Rate Risk

Comptroller's Handbook

Narrative - June 1997, Procedures - March 1998

L

Liquidity and Funds Management

As of January 12, 2012, this guidance applies to federal savings associations in addition to national banks.*

Interest Rate Risk

Table of Contents

Introduction

Interest Rate Risk   Introduction

Background

The acceptance and management of financial risk is inherent to the business of banking and banks' roles as financial intermediaries. To meet the demands of their customers and communities and to execute business strategies, banks make loans, purchase securities, and take deposits with different maturities and interest rates. These activities may leave a bank's earnings and capital exposed to movements in interest rates. This exposure is interest rate risk.

Changes in banks' competitive environment, products, and services have heightened the importance of prudent interest rate risk management. Historically, the interest rate environment for banks has been fairly stable, particularly in the decades following World War II. More recently, interest rates have become more volatile, and banks have arguably become more exposed to such volatility because of the changing character of their liabilities. For example, nonmaturity deposits have lost importance and purchased funds have gained.

Each year, the financial products offered and purchased by banks become more various and complex, and many of these products pose risk to the bank. For example, an asset's option features can, in certain interest rate environments, reduce its cash flows and rates of return. The structure of banks' balance sheets has changed. Many commercial banks have increased their holdings of long-term assets and liabilities, whose values are more sensitive to rate changes. Such changes mean that managing interest rate risk is far more important and complex than it was just a decade ago.

This booklet provides guidance on effective interest rate risk management processes. The nature and complexity of a bank's business activities and overall levels of risk should determine how sophisticated its management of interest rate risk must be. Every well-managed bank, however, will have a process that enables bank management to identify, measure, monitor, and control interest rate risk in a timely and comprehensive manner.

The adequacy and effectiveness of a bank's interest rate risk management are important in determining whether a bank's level of interest rate risk exposure poses supervisory concerns or requires additional capital. The guidance and procedures in this booklet are designed to help bankers and examiners evaluate a bank's interest rate risk management process. These guidelines and procedures incorporate and are consistent with the principles that are outlined in the federal banking agencies' joint policy statement on interest rate risk. (A copy of the policy statement, published jointly by the OCC, Federal Deposit Insurance Corporation, and Board of Governors of the Federal Reserve System, can be found in appendix A of this booklet.)

Definition

Interest rate risk is the risk to earnings or capital arising from movement of interest rates. It arises from differences between the timing of rate changes and the timing of cash flows (repricing risk); from changing rate relationships among yield curves that affect bank activities (basis risk); from changing rate relationships across the spectrum of maturities (yield curve risk); and from interest-rate-related options embedded in bank products (option risk). The evaluation of interest rate risk must consider the impact of complex, illiquid hedging strategies or products, and also the potential impact on fee income that is sensitive to changes in interest rates.

The movement of interest rates affects a bank's reported earnings and book capital by changing

- Net interest income,
- The market value of trading accounts (and other instruments accounted for by market value), and
- Other interest sensitive income and expenses, such as mortgage servicing fees.

Changes in interest rates also affect a bank's underlying economic value. The value of a bank's assets, liabilities, and interest-rate-related, off-balance-sheet contracts is affected by a change in rates because the present value of future cash flows, and in some cases the cash flows themselves, is changed.

In banks that manage trading activities separately, the exposure of earnings and capital to those activities because of changes in market factors is referred to as price risk. Price risk is the risk to earnings or capital arising from changes in the value of portfolios of financial instruments. This risk arises from market-making, dealing, and position-taking activities for interest rate, foreign exchange, equity, and commodity markets.

The same fundamental principles of risk management apply to both interest rate risk and price risk. The guidance and procedures contained in this booklet, however, focus on the interest rate risk arising from a bank's structural (e.g., nontrading) position. For additional guidance on price risk management, examiners should refer to the booklet, "Risk Management of Financial Derivatives."

Banking Activities and Interest Rate Risk

Each financial transaction that a bank completes may affect its interest rate risk profile. Banks differ, however, in the level and degree of interest rate risk they are willing to assume. Some banks seek to minimize their interest rate risk exposure. Such banks generally do not deliberately take positions to benefit from a particular movement in interest rates. Rather, they try to match the maturities and repricing dates of their assets and liabilities. Other banks are willing to assume a greater level of interest rate risk and may choose to take interest rate positions or to leave them open.

Banks will differ on which portfolios or activities they allow position-taking in. Some banks attempt to centralize management of interest rate risk and restrict position-taking to certain "discretionary portfolios" such as their money market, investment, and Eurodollar portfolios. These banks often use a funds transfer pricing system to isolate the interest rate risk management and positioning in the treasury unit of the bank. (See appendix H for further discussion of funds transfer pricing systems.) Other banks adopt a more decentralized approach and let individual profit centers or business lines manage and take positions within specified limits. Some banks choose to confine their interest rate risk positioning to their trading activities. Still others may choose to take or leave open interest rate positions in nontrading books and activities.

A bank can alter its interest rate risk exposure by changing investment, lending, funding, and pricing strategies and by managing the maturities and repricings of these portfolios to achieve a desired risk profile. Many banks also use off-balance-sheet derivatives, such as interest rate swaps, to adjust their interest rate risk profile. Before using such derivatives, bank management should understand the cash flow characteristics of the instruments that will be used and have adequate systems to measure and monitor their performance in managing the bank's risk profile. The "Risk Management of Financial Derivatives" booklet provides more guidance on the use and prudent management of financial derivative products.

From an earnings perspective, a bank should consider the effect of interest rate risk on net income and net interest income in order to fully assess the contribution of noninterest income and operating expenses to the interest rate risk exposure of the bank. In particular, a bank with significant fee income should assess the extent to which that fee income is sensitive to rate changes. From a capital perspective, a bank should consider how intermediate (two years to five years) and long-term (more than five years) positions may affect the bank's future financial performance. Since the value of instruments with intermediate and long maturities can be especially sensitive to interest rate changes, it is important for a bank to monitor and control the level of these exposures.

A bank should also consider how interest rate risk may act jointly with other risks facing the bank. For example, in a rising rate environment, loan customers may not be able to meet interest payments because of the increase in the size of the payment or a reduction in earnings. The result will be a higher level of problem loans. An increase in interest rates exposes a bank with a significant concentration of adjustable rate loans to credit risk. For a bank that is predominately funded with short-term liabilities, a rise in rates may decrease net interest income at the same time credit quality problems are on the increase.

When developing and reviewing a bank's interest rate risk profile and strategy, management should consider the bank's liquidity and ability to access various funding and derivative markets. A bank with ample and stable sources of liquidity may be better able to withstand short-term earnings pressures arising from adverse interest rate movements than a bank that is heavily dependent on wholesale, short-term funding sources that may leave the bank if its earnings deteriorate. A bank that depends solely on wholesale funding may have difficulty replacing existing funds or obtaining additional funds if it has an increasing number of nonperforming loans. A bank that can readily access various money and derivatives markets may be better able to respond quickly to changing market conditions than banks that rely on customer-driven portfolios to alter their interest rate risk positions.

Finally, a bank should consider the fit of its interest rate risk profile with its strategic business plans. A bank that has significant long-term interest rate exposures (such as long-term fixed rate assets funded by short-term liabilities) may be less able to respond to new business opportunities because of depreciation in its asset base.

Board and Senior Management Oversight

Effective board and senior management oversight of the bank's interest rate risk activities is the cornerstone of an effective risk management process. It is the responsibility of the board and senior management to understand the nature and level of interest rate risk being taken by the bank and how that risk fits within the overall business strategies of the bank and the mechanisms used to manage that risk. Effective risk management requires an informed board, capable management, and appropriate staffing.

For its part, a board of directors has four broad responsibilities. It must:

- **Establish and guide the bank's strategic direction and tolerance** for interest rate risk and identify the senior managers who have the authority and responsibility for managing this risk.

- **Monitor the bank's performance and overall interest rate risk profile**, ensuring that the level of interest rate risk is maintained at prudent levels and is supported by adequate capital. In assessing the bank's capital adequacy for interest rate risk, the board should consider the bank's current and potential interest rate risk exposure as well as other risks that may impair the bank's capital, such as credit, liquidity, and transaction risks.

- **Ensure that the bank implements sound fundamental principles** that facilitate the identification, measurement, monitoring, and control of interest rate risk.

- **Ensure that adequate resources are devoted** to interest rate risk management. Effective risk management requires both technical and human resources.

Senior management is responsible for ensuring that interest rate risk is managed for both the long range and day to day. In managing the bank's activities, senior management should:

- **Develop and implement procedures and practices** that translate the board's goals, objectives, and risk tolerances into operating standards that are well understood by bank personnel and that are consistent with the board's intent.

- **Ensure adherence to the lines of authority and responsibility** that the board has established for measuring, managing, and reporting interest rate risk exposures.

- **Oversee the implementation and maintenance of management information and other systems** that identify, measure, monitor, and control the bank's interest rate risk.

- **Establish effective internal controls** over the interest rate risk management process.

Effective Risk Management Process

Effective control of interest rate risk requires a comprehensive risk management process that ensures the timely identification, measurement, monitoring, and control of risk. The formality of this process may vary, depending on the size and complexity of the bank. In many cases, banks may choose to establish and communicate risk management practices and principles in writing. The OCC fully endorses placing these principles in writing to ensure effective communication throughout the bank. If, however, management follows sound fundamental principles and appropriately governs the risk in this area, the OCC does not require a written policy. If sound principles are not effectively practiced or if a bank's interest rate risk management process is complex and cannot be effectively controlled by informal policies, the OCC may require management to establish written policies to formally communicate risk guidelines and controls.

Regardless of the mechanism used, a bank's interest rate risk management procedures or process should establish:

- **Responsibility and authority** for identifying the potential interest rate risk arising from new or existing products or activities; establishing and maintaining an interest rate risk measurement system; formulating and executing strategies; and authorizing policy exceptions.

- **An interest rate risk measurement system.** The bank's risk measurement system should be able to identify and quantify the major sources of a bank's interest rate risk in a timely manner.

- **A system for monitoring and reporting risk exposures.** Senior management and the board, or a committee thereof, should receive reports on the bank's interest rate risk profile at least quarterly, but more frequently if the character and level of the bank's risk requires it. These reports should allow senior management and the board to evaluate the amount of interest rate risk being taken, compliance with established risk limits, and whether management's strategies are appropriate in light of the board's expressed risk tolerance.

- **Risk limits and controls** on the nature and amount of interest rate risk that can be taken. When determining risk exposure limits, senior management should consider the nature of the bank's strategies and activities, its past performance, the level of earnings and capital available to absorb potential losses, and the board's tolerance for risk.

- **Internal control procedures.** The oversight of senior management and the board is critical to the internal control process. In addition to establishing clear lines of authority, responsibilities, and risk limits, management and board should ensure that adequate resources are provided to support risk monitoring, audit, and control functions. The persons or units responsible for risk monitoring and control functions should be separate from the persons or units that create risk exposures. The persons or units may be part of a more general operations, audit, compliance, risk management, or treasury unit. If the risk monitoring and control functions are part of a treasury unit that also has the responsibility and authority to execute investment or hedging strategies to manage the bank's risk exposure, it is particularly important that the bank have a strong internal audit function and sufficient safeguards in place to ensure that all trades are reported to senior management in a timely manner and are consistent with strategies approved by senior management.

Organizational Structures for Managing Interest Rate Risk

The organizational structure used to manage a bank's interest rate risk may vary, depending on the size, scope, and complexity of the bank's activities. At many larger banks, the interest rate risk management function may be centralized in the lead bank or holding company. The OCC encourages the efficiencies and comprehensive perspective that such centralized management can provide and does not require banks employing such a structure to have separate interest rate risk management functions at each affiliate bank. Centralized structures, however, do not absolve the directors at each affiliate bank of their fiduciary responsibilities to ensure the safety and soundness of their institutions and to meet capital requirements. Hence, senior managers responsible for the organization's centralized interest rate risk management should ensure that their actions and the resulting risk profile for the company and affiliate banks reflect the overall risk tolerances expressed by each affiliate's board of directors.

When a bank chooses to adopt a more decentralized structure for its interest rate risk activities, examiners should review and evaluate how the interest rate risk profiles of all material affiliates contribute to the organization's company-wide interest rate risk profile. Such an assessment is important because the risk at individual affiliates may either raise or lower the risk profiles of the national bank.

Asset/Liability Management Committee

A bank's board usually will delegate responsibility for establishing specific interest rate risk policies and practices to a committee of senior managers. This senior management committee is often referred to as the Finance Committee or Asset/Liability Management Committee (ALCO).

The ALCO usually manages the structure of the bank's business and the level of interest rate risk it assumes. It is responsible for ensuring that measurement systems adequately reflect the bank's exposure and that reporting systems adequately communicate relevant information concerning the level and sources of the bank's exposure.

To be effective, the ALCO should include representatives from each major section of the bank that assumes interest rate risk. The ALCOs of some banks include a representative from marketing so that marketing efforts are consistent with the ALCO's view on the structure of the bank's business. However, if the bank uses a funds transfer pricing system to centralize interest rate risk management in the treasury unit, it is less important that each major area of the bank be represented. Committee members should be senior managers with clear lines of authority over the units responsible for establishing and executing interest rate positions. A channel must exist for clear communication of ALCO's directives to these line units. The risk management and strategic planning areas of the bank should communicate regularly to facilitate evaluations of risk arising from future business.

ALCO usually delegates day-to-day operating responsibilities to the treasury unit. In smaller banks, the daily operating responsibilities may be handled by the bank's investment officer. ALCO should establish specific practices and limits governing treasury operations before it makes such delegations. Treasury personnel are typically responsible for managing the bank's discretionary portfolios (such as securities, Eurocurrency, time deposits, domestic wholesale liabilities, and off-balance-sheet interest rate contracts).

The treasury unit (or investment officer) can influence the level of interest rate risk in several ways. For example, the unit may be responsible for implementing the policies of ALCO on short- and long-term positions. Regardless of its specific delegations, treasury or other units responsible for monitoring the bank's risk positions should ensure that reports on the bank's current risk are prepared and provided to ALCO in a timely fashion.

Evaluation of Interest Rate Exposures

Management decisions concerning a bank's interest rate risk exposure should take into account the risk/reward trade-off of interest rate risk positions. Management should compare the potential risk (impact of adverse rate movements) of an interest rate risk position or strategy against the potential reward (impact of favorable rate movements).

To evaluate the potential impact of interest rate risk on a bank's operations, a well-managed bank will consider the affect on both its earnings (the earnings or accounting perspective) and underlying economic value (the economic or capital perspective). Both viewpoints must be assessed to determine the full scope of a bank's interest rate risk exposure, especially if the bank has significant long-term or complex interest rate risk positions.

Earnings Perspective

The earnings perspective considers how interest rate changes will affect a bank's reported earnings. For example, a decrease in earnings caused by changes in interest rates can reduce earnings, liquidity, and capital. This perspective focuses on risk to earnings in the near term, typically the next one or two years. Fluctuations in interest rates generally affect reported earnings through changes in a bank's net interest income.

Net interest income will vary because of differences in the timing of accrual changes (repricing risk), changing rate and yield curve relationships (basis and yield curve risks), and options positions. Changes in the general level of market interest rates also may cause changes in the volume and mix of a bank's balance sheet products. For example, when economic activity continues to expand while interest rates are rising, commercial loan demand may increase while residential mortgage loan growth and prepayments slow.

Changes in the general level of interest rates also may affect the volume of certain types of banking activities that generate fee-related income. For example, the volume of residential mortgage loan originations typically declines as interest rates rise, resulting in lower mortgage origination fees. In contrast, mortgage servicing pools often face slower prepayments when rates are rising because borrowers are less likely to refinance. As a result, fee income and associated economic value arising from mortgage servicing-related businesses may increase or remain stable in periods of moderately rising interest rates.

Declines in the market values of certain instruments may diminish near-term earnings when accounting rules require a bank to charge such declines directly to current income. This risk is referred to as price risk. Banks with large trading account activities generally will have separate measurement and limit systems to manage this risk.

Evaluating interest rate risk solely from an earnings perspective may not be sufficient if a bank has significant positions that are intermediate-term (between two years and five years) or long-term (more than five years). This is because most earnings-at-risk measures consider only a one-year to two-year time frame. As a result, the potential impact of interest rate changes on long-term positions often are not fully captured.

Economic Perspective

The economic perspective provides a measure of the underlying value of the bank's current position and seeks to evaluate the sensitivity of that value to changes in interest rates. This perspective focuses on how the economic value of all bank assets, liabilities, and interest-rate-related, off-balance-sheet instruments change with movements in interest rates. The economic value of these instruments equals the present value of their future cash flows. By evaluating changes in the present value of the contracts that result from a given change in interest rates, one can estimate the change to a bank's economic value (also known as the economic value of equity).

In contrast to the earnings perspective, the economic perspective identifies risk arising from long-term repricing or maturity gaps. By capturing the impact of interest rate changes on the value of all future cash flows, the economic perspective can provide a more comprehensive measurement of interest rate risk than the earnings perspective. The future cash flow projections used to estimate a bank's economic exposure provides a pro forma estimate of the bank's future income generated by its current position. Because changes in economic value indicate the anticipated change in the value of the bank's future cash flows, the economic perspective can provide a leading indicator of the bank's future earnings and capital values. Changes in economic value can also affect the liquidity of bank assets because the cost of selling depreciated assets to meet liquidity needs may be prohibitive.

The growing complexity of many bank products and investments heightens the need to consider the economic perspective of interest rate risk. The financial performance of bank instruments increasingly is linked to pricing and cash flow options embedded within those instruments. The impact of some of these options, such as interest rate caps on adjustable rate mortgages (ARMs) and the prepayment option on fixed rate mortgages, may not be discernable if the impact of interest rate changes is evaluated only over a short-term (earnings perspective) time horizon.

For newly originated products, a short-term horizon may underestimate the impact of caps and prepayment options because loan rates are unlikely to exceed caps during the early life of a loan. In addition, borrowers may be unlikely to refinance until the transaction costs associated with originating a loan have been absorbed. As time passes, however, interest rate caps may become binding or borrowers may be more likely to refinance if market opportunities become favorable.

Similarly, some structured notes offer relatively high initial coupon rates to the investor at the expense of potentially lower-than-market rates of return at future dates. Failure to consider the value of future cash flows under a range of interest rate scenarios may leave the bank with an instrument that under-performs the market or provides a rate of return below the bank's funding costs.

A powerful tool to help manage interest rate risk exposure, the economic perspective often is more difficult to quantify than the earnings perspective. Measuring risk from the economic perspective requires a bank to estimate the future cash flows of all of its financial instruments. Since many retail bank products, such as savings and demand deposits, have uncertain cash flows and indefinite maturities, measuring the risk of these accounts can be difficult and requires the bank to make numerous assumptions. Because of the difficulty of precisely estimating market values for every product, many economic measurement systems track the *relative change* or *sensitivity* of values rather than the *absolute change* in value.

Economic value analysis facilitates risk/reward analysis because it provides a common benchmark (present value) for evaluating instruments with different maturities and cash flow characteristics. Many bankers have found this type of analysis to be useful in decision making and risk monitoring.

Trade-Offs in Managing Earnings and Economic Exposures

When immunizing earnings and economic value from interest rate risk, bank management must make certain trade-offs. When earnings are immunized, economic value becomes more vulnerable, and vice versa. The economic value of equity, like that of other financial instruments, is a function of the discounted net cash flows (profits) it is expected to earn in the future. If a bank has immunized earnings, such that expected earnings remain constant for any change in interest rates, the discounted value of those earnings will be lower if interest rates rise. Hence, although the bank's earnings have been immunized, its economic value will fluctuate with rate changes. Conversely, if a bank fully immunizes its economic value, its periodic earnings must increase when rates rise and decline when interest rates fall.

A simple example illustrates this point. Consider a bank that has $100 million in earning assets and $90 million in liabilities. If the assets are earning 10 percent, the liabilities are earning 8 percent, the cost of equity is 8 percent, and the bank's net noninterest expense (including taxes) totals $2 million, the economic value of the bank is $10 million. One arrives at this value by discounting the net earnings of $0.8 million C $10 million in interest income less $7.2 million in interest expense and $2 million in noninterest expense C as a perpetuity at 8 percent. (A perpetuity is an annuity that pays interest forever. Its present value equals the periodic payment received divided by the discount rate.) If net noninterest expenses are not affected by interest rates, the bank can immunize its net income and net interest income by placing $10 million of its assets in perpetuities and the remainder of assets and all liabilities in overnight funds. If this is done, a general 200 basis point increase in interest rates leaves the bank's net income at $0.8 million. The bank earns $11.8 million on its assets ($10 million perpetuity at 10 percent and $90 million overnight assets at 12 percent) and incurs interest expenses of $9 million ($90 million at 10 percent) and noninterest expenses of $2 million. The economic value of its equity, however, declines to $8 million. (The net earnings of $0.8 million are discounted as a perpetuity at 10 percent).

As a result of this trade-off, many banks that limit the sensitivity of their economic value will not set a zero risk tolerance (i.e., try to maintain current economic value at all costs) but rather will set limits around a range of possible outcomes. In addition, because banks generally have some fixed operating expenses that are not sensitive to changes in interest rates (as in the above example), some banks have determined that their risk-neutral position is a slightly long net asset position. The bank's fixed operating expenses, from a cash flow perspective, are like a long-term fixed rate liability that must be offset or hedged by a long-term fixed rate asset.

(Appendix B provides further illustration of the distinctions between the earnings and economic perspectives.)

Supervisory Review of Interest Rate Risk Management

Examiners should determine the adequacy and effectiveness of a bank's interest rate risk management process, the level and trend of the bank's risk exposure, and the adequacy of its capital relative to its exposure and risk management process.

Examiners should discuss with bank management the major sources of the bank's interest rate risk exposure and evaluate whether the bank's measurement systems provide a sufficient basis for identifying and quantifying the major sources of interest rate exposure. They should also analyze the integrity and effectiveness of the bank's interest rate risk control and management processes to ensure that the bank's practices comply with the stated objectives and risk tolerances of senior management and the board.

In forming conclusions about the safety and soundness of the bank's interest rate risk management and exposures, examiners should consider:

- The complexity and level of risk posed by the assets, liabilities, and off-balance-sheet activities of the bank.
- The adequacy and effectiveness of board and senior management oversight.
- Management's knowledge and ability to identify and manage sources of interest rate risk.
- The adequacy of internal measurement, monitoring, and management information systems.
- The adequacy and effectiveness of risk limits and controls that set tolerances on income and capital losses.
- The adequacy of the bank's internal review and audit of its interest rate
 risk management process.
- The adequacy and effectiveness of the bank's risk management practices and strategies as evidenced in past and projected financial performance.
- The appropriateness of the bank's level of interest rate risk in relation to the bank's earnings, capital, and risk management systems.

At the conclusion of each exam, the examiner should update the bank's risk assessment profile for interest rate risk using the factors and guidance in "Supervision by Risk," a discussion that examiners can find in either of two booklets C "Large Bank Supervision" or A "Community Bank Risk Assessment System." The guidance is reproduced in appendixes C and D. Although examiners should use "Community Bank Procedures for Noncomplex Banks" to evaluate community banks, they should use the expanded procedures contained in "Interest Rate Risk" for community institutions exhibiting high interest rate risk or moderate interest rate risk with increasing exposure. Use these expanded procedures for all large banks.

Capital Adequacy

The OCC expects all national banks to maintain adequate capital for the risks they undertake. The OCC's risk-based and leverage capital standards establish minimum capital thresholds that all national banks must meet (see the *Comptroller's Handbook's* "Capital and Dividends" for additional guidance on capital and the OCC's capital requirements). Many banks may need capital above these minimum standards to adequately cover their activities and aggregate risk profile. When determining the appropriate level of capital, bank management should consider the level of current and potential risks its activities pose and the quality of its risk management processes.

With regard to interest rate risk, examiners should evaluate whether the bank has an earnings and capital base that is sufficient to support the bank's level of short- and long-term interest rate risk exposure and the risk those exposures may pose to the bank's future financial performance. Examiners should consider the following factors:

- **The strength and stability of the bank's earnings stream and the level of income the bank needs to generate and maintain normal business operations.** A high level of exposure is one that could, under a reasonable range of interest rate scenarios, result in the bank reporting losses or curtailing normal dividend and business operations. In such cases, bank management must ensure that it has the capital and liquidity to withstand the possible adverse impact of such events until it can implement corrective action, such as reducing exposures or increasing capital.

- **The level of current and potential depreciation in the bank's underlying economic value due to changes in interest rates.** When a bank has significant unrealized losses in its assets because of interest rate changes (e.g., depreciation in its investment or loan portfolios), examiners should evaluate the impact such depreciation, if recognized, would have on the bank's capital levels and ratios. In making this determination, examiners should consider the degree to which the bank's liabilities or off-balance-sheet positions may offset the asset depreciation. Such offsets may include nonmaturity deposits that bank management can demonstrate represent a stable source of fixed rate funding. Alternatively, the bank may have entered into an interest rate swap contract enabling the bank to pay a fixed rate of interest and receive a floating rate of interest. This type of swap contract essentially transforms the bank's floating rate liabilities into a fixed rate source of funds.

    Examiners should consider a bank to have a high level of exposure if its current or potential change in economic value (based on a reasonable interest rate forecast) would, if recognized, result in the bank's capital ratios falling below the "adequately capitalized" level for prompt corrective action purposes. This situation may require additional supervisory attention. At a minimum, bank management should have in place contingency plans for reducing the bank's exposures, raising additional capital, or both.

- **The bank's exposure to other risks that may impair its capital.** Examiners should consider the entire risk profile of the bank relative to its capital, a subject that is discussed more fully in "Capital and Dividends."

Risk Identification

The systems and processes by which a bank identifies and measures risk should be appropriate to the nature and complexity of the bank's operations. Such systems must provide adequate, timely, and accurate information if the bank is to identify and control interest rate risk exposures.

Interest rate risk may arise from a variety of sources, and measurement systems vary in how thoroughly they capture each type of interest rate exposure. To find the measurement systems that are most appropriate, bank management should first consider the nature and mix of its products and activities. Management should understand the bank's business mix and the risk characteristics of these businesses before it attempts to identify the major sources of the bank's interest rate risk exposure and the relative contribution of each source to the bank's overall interest rate risk profile. Various risk measurement systems can then be evaluated by how well they identify and quantify the bank's major sources of risk exposure.

Repricing or Maturity Mismatch Risk

The interest rate risk exposure of banks can be broken down into four broad categories: repricing or maturity mismatch risk, basis risk, yield curve risk, and option risk. Repricing risk results from differences in the timing of rate changes and the timing of cash flows that occur in the pricing and maturity of a bank's assets, liabilities, and off-balance-sheet instruments. Repricing risk is often the most apparent source of interest rate risk for a bank and is often gauged by comparing the volume of a bank's assets that mature or reprice within a given time period with the volume of liabilities that do so. Some banks intentionally take repricing risk in their balance sheet structure in an attempt to improve earnings. Because the yield curve is generally upward-sloping (long-term rates are higher than short-term rates), banks can often earn a positive spread by funding long-term assets with short-term liabilities. The earnings of such banks, however, are vulnerable to an increase in interest rates that raises its cost of funds.

Banks whose repricing asset maturities are longer than their repricing liability maturities are said to be "liability sensitive," because their liabilities will reprice more quickly. The earnings of a liability-sensitive bank generally increase when interest rates fall and decrease when they rise. Conversely, an asset-sensitive bank (asset repricings shorter than liability repricings) will generally benefit from a rise in rates and be hurt by a fall in rates.

Repricing risk is often, but not always, reflected in a bank's current earnings performance. A bank may be creating repricing imbalances that will not be manifested in earnings until sometime into the future. A bank that focuses only on short-term repricing imbalances may be induced to take on increased interest rate risk by extending maturities to improve yield. When evaluating repricing risk, therefore, it is essential that the bank consider not only near-term imbalances but also long-term ones. Failure to measure and manage material long-term repricing imbalances can leave a bank's future earnings significantly exposed to interest rate movements.

Basis Risk

Basis risk arises from a shift in the relationship of the rates in different financial markets or on different financial instruments. Basis risk occurs when market rates for different financial instruments, or the indices used to price assets and liabilities, change at different times or by different amounts. For example, basis risk occurs when the spread between the three-month Treasury and the three-month London interbank offered rate (Libor) changes. This change affects a bank's current net interest margin through changes in the earned/paid spreads of instruments that are being repriced. It also affects the anticipated future cash flows from such instruments, which in turn affects the underlying net economic value of the bank.

Basis risk can also be said to include changes in the relationship between managed rates, or rates established by the bank, and external rates. For example, basis risk may arise because of differences in the prime rate and a bank's offering rates on various liability products, such as money market deposits and savings accounts.

Because consumer deposit rates tend to lag behind increases in market interest rates, many retail banks may see an initial improvement in their net interest margins when rates are rising. As rates stabilize, however, this benefit may be offset by repricing imbalances and unfavorable spreads in other key market interest rate relationships; and deposit rates gradually catch up to the market. (Many bankers view this lagged and asymmetric pricing behavior as a form of option risk. Whether this behavior is categorized as basis or option risk is not important so long as bank management understands the implications that this pricing behavior will have on the bank's interest rate risk exposure.)

Certain pricing indices have a built-in "lag" feature such that the index will respond more slowly to changes in market interest rates. Such lags may either accentuate or moderate the bank's short-term interest rate exposure. One common index with this feature is the 11th District Federal Home Loan Bank Cost of Funds Index (COFI) used in certain adjustable rate residential mortgage products (ARMs). The COFI index, which is based upon the monthly average interest costs of liabilities for thrifts in the 11th District (California, Arizona, and Nevada), is a composite index containing both short- and long-term liabilities. Because current market interest rates will not be reflected in the index until the long-term liabilities have been repriced, the index generally will lag market interest rate movements.

A bank that holds COFI ARMs funded with three-month consumer deposits may find that, in a rising rate environment, its liability costs are rising faster than the repricing rate on the ARMs. In a falling rate environment, the COFI lag will tend to work in the bank's favor, because the interest received from ARMs adjusts downward more slowly than the bank's liabilities.

Hedging with Derivative Contracts

Some banks use off-balance-sheet derivatives as an alternative to other investments; others use them to manage their earnings or capital exposures. Banks can use off-balance-sheet derivatives to achieve any or all of the following objectives: limit downside earnings exposures, preserve upside earnings potential, increase yield, and minimize income or capital volatility.

Although derivatives can be used to hedge interest rate risk, they expose a bank to basis risk because the spread relationship between cash and derivative instruments may change. For example, a bank using interest rate swaps (priced off Libor) to hedge its Treasury note portfolio may face basis risk because the spread between the swap rate and Treasuries may change.

A bank using off-balance-sheet instruments such as futures, swaps, and options to hedge or alter the interest rate risk characteristics of on-balance-sheet positions needs to consider how the off-balance-sheet contract's cash flows may change with changes in interest rates and in relation to the positions being hedged or altered. Derivative strategies designed to hedge or offset the risk in a balance sheet position will typically use derivative contracts whose cash flow characteristics have a strong correlation with the instrument or position being hedged. The bank will also need to consider the relative liquidity and cost of various contracts, selecting the product that offers the best mix of correlation, liquidity, and relative cost. Even if there is a high degree of correlation between the derivative contract and the position being hedged, the bank may be left with residual basis risk because cash and derivative prices do not always move in tandem. Banks holding large derivative portfolios or actively trading derivative contracts should determine whether the potential exposure presents material risk to the bank's earnings or capital.

Yield Curve Risk

Yield-curve risk arises from variations in the movement of interest rates across the maturity spectrum. It involves changes in the relationship between interest rates of different maturities of the same index or market (e.g., a three-month Treasury versus a five-year Treasury). The relationships change when the shape of the yield curve for a given market flattens, steepens, or becomes negatively sloped (inverted) during an interest rate cycle. Yield curve variation can accentuate the risk of a bank's position by amplifying the effect of maturity mismatches.

Certain types of structured notes can be particularly vulnerable to changes in the shape of the yield curve. For example, the performance of certain types of structured note products, such as dual index notes, is directly linked to basis and yield curve relationships. These bonds have coupon rates that are determined by the difference between market indices, such as the constant-maturity Treasury rate (CMT) and Libor. An example would be a coupon whose rate is based on the following formula: coupon equals 10-year CMT plus 300 basis points less three-month Libor. Since the coupon on this bond adjusts as interest rates change, a bank may incorrectly assume that it will always benefit if interest rates increase. If, however, the increase in three-month Libor exceeds the increase in the 10-year CMT rate, the coupon on this instrument will fall, even if both Libor and Treasury rates are increasing. Banks holding these types of instruments should evaluate how their performance may vary under different yield curve shapes.

Option Risk

Option risk arises when a bank or a bank's customer has the right (not the obligation) to alter the level and timing of the cash flows of an asset, liability, or off-balance-sheet instrument. An option gives the option holder the right to buy (call option) or sell (put option) a financial instrument at a specified price (strike price) over a specified period of time. For the seller (or writer) of an option, there is an obligation to perform if the option holder exercises the option.

The option holder's ability to choose whether to exercise the option creates an asymmetry in an option's performance. Generally, option holders will exercise their right only when it is to their benefit. As a result, an option holder faces limited downside risk (the premium or amount paid for the option) and unlimited upside reward. The option seller faces unlimited downside risk (an option is usually exercised at a disadvantageous time for the option seller) and limited upside reward (if the holder does not exercise the option and the seller retains the premium).

Options often result in an asymmetrical risk/reward profile for the bank. If the bank has written (sold) options to its customers, the amount of earnings or capital value that a bank may lose from an unfavorable movement in interest rates may exceed the amount that the bank may gain if rates move in a favorable direction. As a result, the bank may have more downside exposure than upside reward. For many banks, their written options positions leave them exposed to losses from both rising and falling interest rates.

Some banks buy and sell options on a "stand-alone" basis. The option has an explicit price at which it is bought or sold and may or may not be linked with another bank product. A bank does not have to buy and sell explicitly priced options to incur option risk, however. Indeed, almost all banks incur option risk from options that are embedded or incorporated into retail bank products. These options are found on both sides of the balance sheet.

On the asset side, prepayment options are the most prevalent embedded option. Most residential mortgage and consumer loans give the consumer an option to prepay with little or no prepayment penalty. Banks may also permit the prepayment of commercial loans by not enforcing prepayment penalties (perhaps to remain competitive in certain markets). A prepayment option is equivalent to having written a call option to the customer. When rates decline, customers will exercise the calls by prepaying loans, and the bank's asset maturities will shorten just when the bank would like to be extending them. And when rates rise, customers will keep their mortgages, making it difficult for the bank to shorten asset maturities just when it would like to be doing so.

On the deposit side of the balance sheet, the most prevalent option given to customers is the right of early withdrawal. Early withdrawal rights are like put options on deposits. When rates increase, the market value of the customer's deposit declines, and the customer has the right to "put" the deposit back to the bank. This option is to the depositor's advantage. As previously noted, bank management's discretion in pricing such retail products as nonmaturity deposits can also be viewed as a type of option. This option usually works in the bank's favor. For example, the bank may peg its deposits at rates that lag market rates when interest rates are increasing and that lead market rates when they are decreasing.

Bank products that contain interest "caps" or "floors" are other sources of option risk. Such products are often loans and may have a significant effect on a bank's rate exposure. For the bank, a loan cap is like selling a put option on a fixed income security, and a floor is like owning a call. The cap or floor rate of interest is the strike price. When market interest rates exceed the cap rate, the borrower's option moves Ain the money" because the borrower is paying interest at a rate lower than market. When market interest rates decline below the floor, the bank's option moves Ain the money" because the rate paid on the loan is higher than the market rate.

Floating rate loans that do not have an explicit cap may have an implicit one at the highest rate that the borrower can afford to pay. In high rate environments, the bank may have to cap the rate on the loan, renegotiate the loan to a lower rate, or face a default on the loan. A bank's nonmaturity deposits, such as money market demand accounts (MMDAs), negotiable order of withdrawal (NOW) accounts, and savings accounts also may have implicit caps and floors on the rates of interest that the bank is willing to pay.

Risk Measurement

Accurate and timely measurement of interest rate risk is necessary for proper risk management and control. A bank's risk measurement system should be able to identify and quantify the major sources of the bank's interest rate risk exposure. The system also should enable management to identify risks arising from the bank's customary activities and new businesses. The nature and mix of a bank's business lines and the interest rate risk characteristics of its activities will dictate the type of measurement system required. Such systems will vary from bank to bank.

Every risk measurement system has limitations, and systems vary in the degree to which they capture various components of interest rate exposure. Many well-managed banks will use a variety of systems to fully capture all of their sources of interest rate exposure. The three most common risk measurement systems used to quantify a bank's interest rate risk exposure are repricing maturity gap reports, net income simulation models, and economic valuation or duration models. The following table summarizes the types of interest rate exposures that these measurement techniques address.

Interest Rate Risk Models

	Gap Report	Earnings Simulation	Economic Valuation
Short-Term Earnings Exposure	Yes	Yes	Generally does not distinguish short-term accounting earnings from changes in economic value.
Long-Term Exposure	Yes	Limited*	Yes
Repricing Risk	Yes	Yes	Yes
Basis Risk	Limited*	Yes	Limited*
Yield Curve Risk	Limited*	Yes	Yes
Option risk	Limited*	Limited*	Yes

* The ability of these types of models to capture this type of risk will vary with the sophistication of the model and the manner in which bank management uses them.

Banks with significant option risk may supplement these models with option pricing or Monte Carlo models. But for many banks, especially smaller ones, the expense of developing options pricing models would outweigh the benefits. Such banks should be able to use their data and measurement systems to identify and track, in a timely and meaningful manner, products that may create significant option risk. Such products may include nonmaturity deposits, loans and securities with prepayment and extension risk, and explicit and embedded caps on adjustable rate loans. Bank management should understand how such options may alter the bank's interest rate exposure under various interest rate environments.

(Appendix E provides background information on each of these types of models. Appendix F discusses factors that bank management should consider when determining whether to purchase or develop internally an interest rate risk measurement system.)

Regardless of the type and level of complexity of a bank's measurement system, management should ensure that the system is adequate to the task. All measurement systems require a bank to gather and input position data, make assumptions about possible future interest rate environments and customer behavior, and compute and quantify risk exposure. To assess the adequacy of a bank's interest rate risk measurement process, examiners should review and evaluate each of these steps.

Gathering Data

The first step in a bank's risk measurement process is to gather data to describe the bank's current financial position. Every measurement system, whether it is a gap report or a complex economic value simulation model, requires information on the composition of the bank's current balance sheet.

In modeling terms, gathering financial data is sometimes called "providing the current position inputs." This data must be reliable for the risk measurement system to be useful. The bank should have sufficient management information systems (MIS) to allow it to retrieve appropriate and accurate information in a timely manner. The MIS systems should capture interest rate risk data on all of the bank's material positions, and there should be sufficient documentation of the major data sources used in the bank's risk measurement process.

Bank management should be alert to the following common data problems of interest rate risk measurement systems:

- Incomplete data on the bank's operations, portfolios, or branches.
- Lack of information on off-balance-sheet positions and on caps and floors incorporated into bank loan and deposit products.
- Inappropriate levels of data aggregation.

Information to Be Collected

To describe the interest rate risk inherent in the bank's current position, the bank should have, for every material type of financial instrument or portfolio, information on:

- The current balance and contractual rate of interest associated with the instrument or portfolio.
- The scheduled or contractual terms of the instrument or portfolio in terms of principal payments, interest reset dates, and maturities.
- For adjustable rate items, the rate index used for repricing (such as prime, Libor, or CD) as well as whether the instruments have contractual interest rate ceilings or floors.

A bank may need to collect additional information on certain products to provide a more complete picture of the bank's interest rate risk exposure. For example, because the age or "seasoning" of certain loans, such as mortgages, may affect their prepayment speeds, the bank may need to obtain information on the origination date and interest rate of the instruments. The geographic location of the loan or deposit may also help the bank evaluate prepayment or withdrawal speeds.

Some banks may use a "tiered" pricing structure for certain products such as consumer deposits. Under such pricing structures, the level and responsiveness of the rates offered for deposits will vary by the size of the deposit account. If the bank uses this type of pricing, it may need to stratify certain portfolios by account size.

Since a bank's interest rate risk exposure extends beyond its on-balance-sheet positions to include off-balance-sheet interest contracts and rate-sensitive fee income, the bank should include these items in its interest rate risk measurement process.

Sources of Information

To obtain the detailed information necessary to measure interest rate risk, banks need to be able to tap or "extract" data from numerous and diverse transaction systems C the base systems that keep the records of each transaction's maturity, pricing, and payment terms. This means that the bank will need to access information from a variety of systems, including its commercial and consumer loan, investment, and deposit systems. The bank's general ledger may also be used to check the integrity of balance information pulled from these transaction systems. Information from the general ledger system by itself, however, generally will not contain sufficient information on the maturity and repricing characteristics of the bank's portfolios.

Aggregation

The amount of data aggregated from transaction systems for the interest rate risk model will vary from bank to bank and from portfolio to portfolio within a bank. Some banks may input each specific instrument for certain portfolios. For example, the cash flow characteristics of certain complex CMO or structured notes may be so transaction-specific that a bank elects to model or input each transaction separately. More typically, the bank will perform some preliminary data aggregation before putting the data into its interest rate risk model. This ensures ease of use and computing efficiency. Although most bank models can handle hundreds of "accounts" or transactions, every model has its limit.

Because some portfolios contain numerous variables that can affect their interest rate risk, additional categories of information or less aggregated information may be required. For example, banks with significant holdings of adjustable rate mortgages will need to differentiate balances by periodic and lifetime caps, the reset frequency of mortgages, and the market index used for rate resets. Banks with significant holdings of fixed rate mortgages will need to stratify balances by coupon levels to reflect differences in prepayment behaviors.

Developing Scenarios and Assumptions

The second step in a bank's interest rate risk measurement process is to project future interest rate environments and to measure the risk to the bank in these environments by determining how certain influences (cash flows, market and product interest rates) will act together to change prices and earnings. Unlike the first step, in which one can be "certain" about data inputs, here the bank must make assumptions about future events. For the risk measurement system to be reliable, these assumptions must be sound.

A bank's interest rate risk exposure is largely a function of (1) the sensitivity of the bank's instruments to a given change in market interest rates and (2) the magnitude and direction of this change in market interest rates. The assumptions and interest rate scenarios developed by the bank in this step are usually shaped by these two variables.

Some common problems in this step of the risk measurement process include:

- Failing to assess potential risk exposures over a sufficiently wide range of interest rate movements to identify vulnerabilities and stress points.

- Failing to modify or vary assumptions for products with embedded options to be consistent with individual rate scenarios.

- Basing assumptions solely on past customer behavior and performance without considering how the bank's competitive market and customer base may change in the future.

- Failing to periodically reassess the reasonableness and accuracy of assumptions.

Future Interest Rate Assumptions

A bank must determine the range of potential interest rate movements over which it will measure its exposure. Bank management should ensure that risk is measured over a reasonable range of potential rate changes, including meaningful stress situations. In developing appropriate rate scenarios, bank management should consider a variety of factors such as the shape and level of the current term structure of interest rates and the historical and implied volatility of interest rates. The bank should also consider the nature and sources of its risk exposure, the time it would realistically need to take actions to reduce or unwind unfavorable risk positions, and bank management's willingness to recognize losses in order to reposition its risk profile. Banks should select scenarios that provide meaningful estimates of risk and include sufficiently wide ranges to allow management to understand the risk inherent in the bank's products and activities.

Banks should use interest rate scenarios with at least a 200-basis-point change taking place in one year. Since 1984, rates have twice changed that much or more in that period of time. The OCC encourages banks to assess the impact of both immediate and gradual changes in market rates as well as changes in the shape of the yield curve when evaluating their risk exposure. The OCC also encourages banks to employ "stress tests" that consider changes of 400 basis points or more over a one-year horizon. Although such a shock is at the upper end of post-1984 experience, it was typical between 1979 and 1984.

Banks with significant option risk should include scenarios that capture the exercise of such options. For example, banks that have products with caps or floors should include scenarios that assess how the bank's risk profile would change should those caps or floors become binding. Some banks write large, explicitly priced interest rate options. Since the market value of options fluctuates with changes in the volatility of rates as well as with changes in the level of rates, such banks should also develop interest rate risk assumptions to measure their exposure to changes in volatility.

Developing Rate Scenarios

The method used to develop specific rate scenarios will vary from bank to bank. In building a rate scenario, the bank will need to specify:

- The term structure of interest rates that will be incorporated in its rate scenario.

- The "basis" relationships between yield curves and rate indices C for example, the spreads between Treasury, Libor, and CD rates.

The bank also must estimate how rates that are administered or managed by bank management (as opposed to those that are purely market driven) might change. Administered rates, which often move more slowly than market rates, including rates such as the bank's prime rate, and rates it pays on consumer deposits.

From these specifications, the bank develops interest rate scenarios over which exposures will be measured. The complexity of the actual scenarios used may range from a simple assumption that all rates move simultaneously in a parallel fashion to more complex rate scenarios involving multiple yield curves. Banks will generally use one of two methods to develop interest rate scenarios:

- The *deterministic* approach. Using this common method, the bank specifies the amount and timing of the rate changes to be evaluated. The risk modeler is determining in advance the range of potential rate movements. Banks using this approach will typically establish standard scenarios for their risk analysis and reporting, based on estimates of the likelihood of adverse interest rate movements. The bank may also include an analysis of its exposure under a "most likely" or flat rate scenario for comparative purposes. These standard rate scenarios are then supplemented periodically with "stress test" scenarios.

The number of scenarios used may range from three (flat, up, down) to 40 or more. These scenarios may include "rate shocks," in which rates are assumed to move instantaneously to a new level, and "rate ramps," where rates move more gradually. Banks may use parallel and nonparallel yield curve shifts, with tests for yield curve twists or inversions.

Models using deterministic rate scenarios generate an indicator of risk exposure for each rate scenario by highlighting the difference in net income between the base case and other scenarios. For example, the model may estimate the level of net income over the next 12 months for each rate scenario. Results often are displayed in a matrix-type table with exposures for base, high, and low rate scenarios.

- The *stochastic* approach. Developed out of options and mortgage-pricing applications, this method employs a model to randomly generate interest rate scenarios, and thousands of individual interest rate scenarios or paths are evaluated. Models using this approach generate a distribution of outcomes or exposures. Banks use these distributions to estimate the probabilities of a certain range of outcomes. For example, the bank may want to have 95 percent confidence that the bank's net income over the next 12 months will not decline by more than a certain amount.

Behavioral and Pricing Assumptions

When assessing its interest rate risk exposure, a bank also must make judgments and assumptions about how an instrument's actual maturity or repricing behavior may vary from the instrument's contractual terms. For example, customers can change the contractual terms of an instrument by prepaying loans, making various deposit withdrawals, or closing deposit accounts (deposit runoffs). The bank must assess the likelihood that customers will elect to exercise these options. These likelihoods will generally vary with each interest rate scenario. In addition, a bank's vulnerability to customers exercising embedded options in retail assets and liabilities will vary from bank to bank because of differences in customer bases and demographics, competition, pricing, and business philosophies.

Assumptions are especially important for products that have unspecified repricing dates, such as demand deposits, savings, NOW and MMDA accounts (nonmaturity deposits), and credit card loans. Management must estimate the date on which these balances will reprice, migrate to other bank products, or run off. In doing so, bank management needs to consider many factors such as the current level of market interest rates and the spread between the bank's offering rate and market rates; its competition from banks and other firms; its geographic location and the demographic characteristics of its customer base. (See appendix F for a more detailed discussion of nonmaturity deposit assumptions.)

A bank's assumptions need to be consistent and reasonable for each interest rate scenario used. For example, assumptions about mortgage prepayments should vary with the rate scenario and reflect a customer's economic incentives to prepay the mortgage in that interest rate environment. A bank should avoid selecting assumptions that are arbitrary and not verified by experience and performance. Typical information sources used to help formulate assumptions include:

- Historical trend analysis of past portfolio and individual account behavior.

- Bank- or vendor-developed prepayment models.

- Dealer or vendor estimates.

- Managerial and business unit input about business and pricing strategies.

Bank management should ensure that key assumptions are evaluated at least annually for reasonableness. Market conditions, competitive environments, and strategies change over time, causing assumptions to lose their validity. For example, if the bank's competitive market has changed such that consumers now face lower transaction costs for refinancing their residential mortgages, prepayments may be triggered by smaller reductions in market interest rates than in the past. Similarly, as bank products go through their life cycle, bank management's business and pricing strategies for the product may change.

A bank's review of key assumptions should include an assessment of the impact of those assumptions on the bank's measured exposure. This type of assessment can be done by performing "what-if" or sensitivity analyses that examine what the bank's exposure would be under a different set of assumptions. By conducting such analyses, bank management can determine which assumptions are most critical and deserve more frequent monitoring or more rigorous methods to ensure their reasonableness. These analyses also serve as a type of stress test that can help management to ensure that the bank's safety and soundness would not be impaired if future events vary from management's expectations.

Management should document the types of analyses underlying key assumptions. Such documents, which usually briefly describe the types of analyses, facilitate the periodic review of assumptions. It also helps to ensure that more than one person in the organization understands how assumptions are derived. The volume and detail of that documentation should be consistent with the significance of the risk and the complexity of analysis. For a small bank, the documentation typically will include an analysis of historical account behavior and comments about pricing strategies, competitor considerations, and relevant economic factors. Larger banks often use more rigorous and statistically based analyses. The bank's key assumptions and their impact should be reviewed by the board, or a committee thereof, at least annually.

Computing Risk Levels

The third step in a bank's risk measurement process is the calculation of risk exposure. Data on the bank's current position is used in conjunction with its assumptions about future interest rates, customer behavior, and business activities to generate expected maturities, cash flows, or earnings estimates, or all three. The manner in which risk is quantified will depend on the methods of measuring risk.

Appendix E discusses commonly used measurement systems and how they quantify risk exposure.

Some banks encounter the following problems when using risk measurement systems:

- The model no longer captures all material sources of a bank's interest rate risk exposure. Banks that have not updated risk measurement techniques for changes in business strategies and products or acquisition and merger activities can experience this problem.

- Bank management does not understand the model's methods and assumptions. Banks that purchase a vendor model and fail to obtain current user guides and source documents that describe the model's implied assumptions and calculation methods may misinterpret model results or have difficulties with the measurement system.

- Only one person in the bank is able to run and maintain the risk measurement system. Should that person leave the bank, the institution may not be able to generate timely and accurate estimates of its risk exposure. More than one person, when possible, should have detailed knowledge of the measurement system.

Calculating Risk to Reported Earnings

The OCC expects all national banks to have systems that enable them to measure the amount of earnings that may be at risk from changes in interest rates. Calculating a bank's reported earnings-at-risk is the focus of many commonly used interest rate risk models. When measuring risk to earnings, these models typically focus on:

- Net interest income, or the risk to earnings arising from accrual accounts. This part of a bank's interest rate risk model is similar to a budget or forecasting model. The model multiplies projected average rates by projected average balances. The projected average rates and balances are derived from the bank's current positions and its assumptions about future interest rates, maturities and repricings of existing positions, and new business assumptions.

- Mark-to-market gains or losses on trading or dealing positions (i.e., price risk). This calculation is often performed in a separate market valuation model or subsystem of the interest rate risk model. In essence, these models project all expected future cash flows and then discount them back to a present value. The model measures exposure by calculating the change in net present values under different interest rate scenarios.

Rate-sensitive fee income, or the risk to earnings arising from interest sensitive fee income or operating expenses. Examples include mortgage servicing fees and income arising from credit card securitization.

Calculating Risk to Capital

Banks that have significant medium- and long-term positions should be able to assess the long-term impact of changes in interest rates on the earnings and capital of the bank. Such an assessment affords the economic perspective or EVE. The appropriate method for assessing a bank's long-term exposures will depend on the maturity and complexity of the bank's assets, liabilities, and off-balance-sheet activities. That method could be a gap report covering the full maturity range of the bank's activities, a system measuring the economic value of equity, or a simulation model.

To determine whether a bank needs a system that measures the impact of long-term positions on capital, examiners should consider the bank's balance sheet structure and its exposure to option risk. For example, a bank with more than 25 percent of total assets in long-term, fixed rate securities and comparatively little in nonmaturity deposits or long-term funding may need to measure the long-term impact on the economic value of equity. If a bank is invested mainly in short-term securities and working capital loans and funded chiefly by short-term deposits, it probably would not.

Banks can measure the volatility of long-term interest rate risk exposures using a variety of methods. For example, a bank that is considerably exposed to intermediate-term (three to five years) interest rate risk may elect to expand its earnings-at-risk analysis beyond the traditional one- to two-year time period. Gap reports that reflect a variety of rate scenarios and that provide sufficient detail in the timing of long-term mismatches may also be used to measure long-term interest rate risk.

The OCC encourages banks with significant interest rate risk exposures to augment their earnings-at-risk measures with systems that can quantify the potential effect of changes in interest rates on their economic value of equity. With few exceptions, larger national banks engaging in complex on- and off-balance-sheet activities need such measurement systems.

To quantify its economic value of equity exposure, a bank generally will use either duration-based models (where duration is a proxy for market value sensitivity) or market (economic) valuation models. These models are essentially a collection of present value calculations that discount the cash flows derived from the current position and assumptions for a specified interest rate scenario.

Static discounted cash flow models are associated with deterministic models. In deterministic models, the user designates an interest rate scenario, and the model generates an exposure estimate for the scenario. Stochastic models use rate scenarios that are randomly generated. Exposure estimates are then generated for each scenario, and an estimate of expected value can be calculated from the distribution of estimates.

Although stochastic models require more expertise and computing power than deterministic models, they provide more accurate risk estimates. Specifically, stochastic models produce more accurate estimates for options and products with embedded options. The value of most options increases continually as interest rates approach the option's strike rates, and the probability of the option going Ainto the money" likewise increases continually. Stochastic models capture this effect because they calculate an expected value of future cash flows derived from a distribution of rate paths. Deterministic models, in contrast, view an option unrealistically as riskless until the predetermined rate path rises above the strike price, at which point the exposure estimate suddenly becomes very large.

Risk Monitoring

Interest rate risk management is a dynamic process. Measuring the interest rate exposure of current business is not enough; a bank should also estimate the effect of new business on its exposure. Periodically, institutions should re-evaluate whether current strategies are appropriate for the bank's desired risk profile. Senior management and the board should have reporting systems that enable them to monitor the bank's current and potential risk exposure and to ensure that those levels are consistent with their stated objectives.

Evaluating and Implementing Strategies

Well-managed banks look not only at the risk arising from their existing business but also at exposures that could arise from expected business growth. In their risk-to-earnings analyses, they may make assumptions about the type and mix of activities and businesses as well as the volume, pricing, and maturities of future business. Typically, strategic business plans, marketing strategies, annual budgets, and historical trend analyses help banks to formulate these assumptions. Some banks may also include new business assumptions in analyzing the risk to the bank's economic value. To do so, a bank first quantifies the sensitivity of its economic value of equity (EVE) to the risks posed by its current positions. Then it recomputes its EVE sensitivity as of a future date, under a projected or pro forma balance sheet.

Although new business assumptions introduce yet another subjective factor to the risk measurement process, they help bank management to anticipate future risk exposures. When incorporating assumptions about new and changing business mix, bank management should ensure that those assumptions are realistic for the rate scenario being evaluated and are attainable given the bank's competition and overall business strategies. In particular, bank management should avoid overly optimistic assumptions that serve to mask the bank's interest rate exposure arising from its existing business mix. For example, to improve its earnings under a rising interest rate scenario, bank management may want to increase the volume of its floating rate loans and decrease its fixed rate loans. Such a restructuring, however, may take considerable time and effort, given the bank's overall lending strategies, customer base, and customer preferences.

Larger banks typically monitor their interest rate risk exposure frequently and develop strategies to adjust their risk exposures. These adjustments may be decisions to buy or sell specific instruments or from certain portfolios, strategic decisions for business lines, maturity or pricing strategies, and hedging or risk transformation strategies using derivative instruments. The bank's interest rate risk model may be used to test or evaluate strategies before implementation. Special subsystems or models may be employed to analyze specific instruments or strategies, such as derivative transactions. The results from these models are entered into the overall interest rate risk model.

Examiners should review and discuss with bank management how the bank evaluates potential interest rate risk exposures of new products or future business plans. Examiners should assess whether the bank's assumptions about new business are realistic and attainable. In addition, examiners should review the bank's interest rate risk strategies to determine whether they meet or are consistent with the stated goals and objectives of senior management and the board.

Interest Rate Risk Reporting

Banks should have an adequate system for reporting risk exposures. A bank's senior management and its board or a board committee should receive reports on the bank's interest rate risk profile at least quarterly. More frequent reporting may be appropriate depending on the bank's level of risk and the likelihood of its level of risk changing significantly. These reports should allow senior management and the board or committee to do the following:

- Evaluate the level and trends of aggregate interest rate risk exposure.

- Evaluate the sensitivity of key assumptions, such as those dealing with changes in the shape of the yield curve or in the speed of anticipated loan prepayments or deposit withdrawals.

- Evaluate the trade-offs between risk levels and performance. When management considers major interest rate strategies (including no action), they should assess the impact of potential risk (an adverse rate movement) against that of the potential reward (a favorable rate movement).

- Verify compliance with the board's established risk tolerance levels and limits and identify any policy exceptions.

- Determine whether the bank holds sufficient capital for the level of interest rate risk being taken.

The reports provided to the board and senior management should be clear, concise, and timely and provide the information needed for making decisions. Reports to the board should also cover control activities. Such reports include (but are not limited to) audit reports, independent valuations of products used for interest rate risk management (e.g., derivatives, investment securities), and model validations comparing model predictions to performance.

Risk Control

A bank's internal control structure ensures the safe and sound functioning of the organization generally and of its interest rate risk management process in particular. Establishing and maintaining an effective system of controls, including the enforcement of official lines of authority and appropriate separation of duties, is one of management's more important responsibilities. Persons responsible for evaluating risk monitoring and control procedures should be independent of the function they review.

Key elements of the control process include internal review and audit and an effective risk limit structure.

Auditing the Interest Rate Risk Measurement Process

Banks need to review and validate each step of the interest rate risk measurement process for integrity and reasonableness. This review is often performed by a number of different units in the organization, including ALCO or treasury staff (regularly and routinely), and a risk control unit that has oversight responsibility for interest rate risk modeling. Internal and external auditors also can periodically review a bank's process. At smaller banks, external auditors or consultants often perform this function.

Examiners should identify the units or individuals responsible for auditing important steps in the interest rate risk measurement process. The examiner should review recent internal or external audit work papers and assess the sufficiency of audit review and coverage. The examiner should determine in particular whether an appropriate level of senior management or staff periodically reviews and validates the assumptions and structure of the bank's interest rate risk measurement process. Management or staff performing these reviews should be sufficiently independent from the line units or individuals who take or create interest rate risk.

Among the items that an audit should review and validate are:

- **The appropriateness of the bank's risk measurement system(s) given the nature, scope, and complexity of its activities.**

- **The accuracy and completeness of the data inputs into the model.** This includes verifying that balances and contractual terms are correctly specified and that all major instruments, portfolios, and business units are captured in the model. The review also should investigate whether data extracts and model inputs have been reconciled with transactions and general ledger systems. It is acceptable for parts of the reconcilement to be automated; e.g, routines may be programmed to investigate whether the balances being extracted from various transaction systems match the balances recorded on the bank's general ledger. Similarly, the model itself often contains various audit checks to ensure, for example, that maturing balances do not exceed original balances. More detailed, periodic audit tests of specific portfolios may also be performed by ALCO, audit staffs, or both.

- **The reasonableness and validity of scenarios and assumptions.** The audit function should review the appropriateness of the interest rate scenarios as well as customer behaviors and pricing/volume relationships to ensure that these assumptions are reasonable and internally consistent. For example, the level of projected mortgage prepayments within a scenario should be consistent with the level of interest rates used in that scenario. Generally this will mean using faster prepayment rates in declining interest rates scenarios and slower prepayment rates in rising rate scenarios. An audit should review the statistical methods that were used to generate scenarios and assumptions (if applicable), and whether senior management reviewed and approved key assumptions.

  The audit or review also should compare actual pricing spreads and balance sheet behavior to model assumptions. For some instruments, such as residential mortgage loans, estimates of value changes can be compared with market value changes. Unfavorable results may lead the bank to revise model relationships such as prepayment and pricing behaviors.

- **The validity of the risk measurement calculations.** The validity of the model calculations is often tested by comparing actual with forecasted results. When doing so, banks will typically compare projected net income results with actual earnings. Reconciling the results of economic valuation systems can be more difficult because market prices for all instruments are not always readily available, and the bank does not routinely mark all of its balance sheet to market. For instruments or portfolios with market prices, these prices are often used to benchmark or check model assumptions.

  The scope and formality of the measurement validation will depend on the size and complexity of the bank. At large banks, internal and external auditors may have their own models against which the bank's model is tested. Larger banks and banks with more complex risk profiles and measurement systems should have the model or calculations audited or validated by an independent source C either an internal risk control unit of the bank, auditors, or consultants. At smaller and less complex banks, periodic comparisons of actual performance with forecasts may be sufficient.

Risk Limits

The bank's board of directors should set the bank's tolerance for interest rate risk and communicate that tolerance to senior management. Based on these tolerances, senior management should establish appropriate risk limits that maintain a bank's exposure within the board's risk tolerances over a range of possible changes in interest rates. Limit controls should ensure that positions that exceed predetermined levels receive prompt management attention.

A bank's limits should be consistent with its overall approach to measuring interest rate risk and should be based on its capital levels, earnings performance, and risk tolerance. The limits should be appropriate to the size, complexity, and capital adequacy of the bank and address the potential impact of changes in market interest rates on both reported earnings and the bank's economic value of equity (EVE).

Many banks will use a combination of limits to control their interest rate risk exposures. These limits include primary limits on the level of reported earnings at risk and economic value at risk (for example, the amount by which net income and economic value may change for a given interest rate scenario) as well as "secondary" limits. These secondary limits form a "second line of defense" and include more traditional volume limits for maturities, coupons, markets, or instruments.

The creation of interest rate risk exposures may also be controlled by pricing policies and internal funds transfer pricing systems. Funds transfer systems typically require line units to obtain funding prices from the bank's treasury unit for large transactions. Those funding prices generally reflect the cost that the bank would incur to hedge or match-fund the transaction. (Appendix H provides additional information on funds transfer pricing systems.)

Examiners should identify and evaluate the types of limits the bank uses to control the risk to earnings and capital from changes in interest rates. In particular, the examiner should determine whether the risk limits are effective methods for controlling the bank's exposure and complying with the board's expressed risk tolerances. The examiner also should assess the appropriateness of the level of risk allowed under the bank's risk limits in view of the bank's financial condition, the quality of its risk management practices and managerial expertise, and its capital base.

Earnings-At-Risk Limits

Earnings-at-risk limits are designed to control the exposure of a bank's projected future reported earnings in specified rate scenarios. A limit is usually expressed as a change in projected earnings (in dollars or percent) over a specified time horizon and rate scenario. Banks typically compute their earnings-at-risk limits relative to one of the following target accounts: net interest income (NII), pre-provision net income (PPNI), net income (NI), or earnings per share (EPS).

The appropriate target account may vary and generally depends upon the nature and sources of the bank's earnings exposure. For some banks, most if not all of their earnings volatility will occur in their net interest margin. For these banks, NII may be an appropriate target. In constructing a limit based on NII, however, bank management should consider and understand how variations in its margin may affect its bottom-line earnings performance. A bank with substantial overhead expenses, for example, may find that relatively small variations in its margin result in significant changes to its net income.

Banks with significant noninterest income and expense items that are sensitive to interest rates generally should consider a more bottom-line-oriented targeted account, such as NI or EPS.

Capital-At-Risk (EVE) Limits

A bank's EVE limits should reflect the size and complexity of its underlying positions. For banks with few holdings of complex instruments and low risk profiles, simple limits on permissible holdings or allowable repricing mismatches in intermediate- and long-term instruments may be adequate. At more complex institutions, more extensive limit structures may be necessary. Banks that have significant intermediate- and long-term mismatches or complex options positions should establish limits to restrict possible losses of economic value or capital.

Gap Limits

Gap (maturity or repricing) limits are designed to reduce the potential exposure to a bank's earnings or capital from changes in interest rates. The limits control the volume or amount of repricing imbalances in a given time period.

These limits often are expressed by the ratio of rate-sensitive assets (RSA) to rate-sensitive liabilities (RSL) in a given time period. A ratio greater than one suggests that the bank is asset-sensitive and has more assets than liabilities subject to repricing. All other factors being constant, the earnings of such a bank generally will be reduced by falling interest rates. An RSA/RSL ratio less than one means that the bank is liability-sensitive and that its earnings may be reduced by rising interest rates. Other gap limits that banks use to control exposure include gap-to-assets ratios, gap-to-equity ratios, and dollar limits on the net gap.

Although gap ratios may be a useful way to limit the volume of a bank's repricing exposures, the OCC does not believe that, by themselves, they are an adequate or effective method of communicating the bank's risk profile to senior management or the board. Gap limits are not estimates of the earnings (net interest income) that the bank has at risk. A bank that relies solely on gap measures to control its interest rate exposure should explain to its senior management and board the level of earnings and capital at risk that are implied by its gap exposures (imbalances).

(See appendix E for further discussion of gap reports and ratios.)

Interest Rate Risk   Examination Procedures

General Procedures

Many of the steps in these procedures require examiners to gather or review information located throughout the bank, such as in the loans, investments, deposits, and off-balance sheet derivative products areas. To avoid duplicating examination procedures already being performed in these areas, examiners should discuss and share examination data on interest rate risk as well as other pertinent risks, including credit, price, liquidity, and strategic risk, before beginning these procedures.

Examiners should cross-reference information obtained from other areas in working papers. When information is not available from other examiners, it should be requested directly from the bank. The final decision on the scope of the examination and the most appropriate way to obtain information without unduly burdening the bank rests with the examiner-in-charge (EIC).

Objective: To determine the scope of the examination of interest rate risk.

1. Review the following documents to identify any previous problems that require follow-up:

   ☐ Prior examination report comments addressing interest rate risk.
   ☐ Most recent risk assessment profile of the bank.
   ☐ Internal/external audits addressing the interest rate risk management process and working papers if necessary.

2. Obtain and review the following information to form an initial impression of the interest rate risk exposure of the bank and determine whether any material changes have occurred in the structure of the bank's balance sheet or the nature of off-balance sheet activities since the prior examination:

   ☐ Most recent quarterly interest rate risk filter for the bank.
   ☐ Balance sheet and income statement.
   ☐ Investment trial balance and list of investment purchases and sales since the last examination.
   ☐ Budget and variance reports.
   ☐ Most recent board packet and meeting minutes.
   ☐ Minutes of the Asset/Liability Committee meetings since the last examination.

3. Review the UBPR, BERT, and other applicable reports and analyze trends in the bank's quarterly net interest margins since the last examination and annual net interest margins over the previous two years. Assess these margins in the context of the interest rate environments of the corresponding time periods. Analyze trends in the bank's volume, rate, and mix variances to determine whether there have been significant changes in the bank's portfolio composition or in its earnings performance that may signal a change in the bank's current or potential interest rate risk profile.

4. Obtain and review any reports that management uses to identify, measure, monitor, or control interest rate risk. Consider:

   ☐ Simulation model output.
   ☐ Gap reports.
   ☐ Model validation reports.
   ☐ Stress test reports.

5. Determine, during early discussion with management:

- The risk measurement method management uses to calculate and monitor interest rate risk. (Measurement systems may include gap reports, simulation models, and economic value of equity models.)
- Whether management has implemented significant changes in the bank's interest rate risk strategies or exposures.
- The staffing and organization of the ALCO, treasury, investment, and funds management units of the bank.

6.   If the bank is part of a multibank holding company, determine whether the company's organizational structure and its risk management process facilitate a consolidated assessment of the company's aggregate level of risk.

7.   Based on results from the previous steps and discussions with the bank EIC and other appropriate supervisors, determine the scope of this examination.

Select from among the following procedures the steps necessary to meet the examination objectives. It will seldom be necessary to perform all of the steps in an examination.

Quantity of Risk

Conclusion: The quantity of interest rate risk is (low, moderate, high).

Objective: To identify the major sources of interest rate risk assumed by the bank and those areas potentially exposed to significant interest rate risk.

1.   Review and analyze the bank's balance sheet structure, off-balance sheet activities, and trends in its balance sheet composition to identify the major sources of interest rate risk exposures. Consider:

- The maturity and repricing structures of the bank's loans, investments, liabilities, and off-balance sheet items.
- Whether the bank has substantial holdings of products with explicit or embedded options, such as prepayment options, caps, or floors, or products whose rates will considerably lag market interest rates.
- The various indices used by the bank to price its variable rate products (e.g., prime, Libor, Treasury) and the level or mix of products tied to these indices.
- The use and nature of derivative products.
- Other off-balance sheet items (e.g., letters of credit, loan commitments).

2.   Assess and discuss with management the bank's vulnerability to various movements in market interest rates including:

- The timing of interest rate changes and cash flows because of maturity or repricing mismatches.
- Changes in key spread or basis relationships.
- Changes in yield curve relationships.
- The nature and level of embedded options exposures.

Objective: To determine the level of exposure in the areas identified as potentially having significant interest rate risk.

Loan Portfolios

1.   If the bank has substantial volumes of loans with unspecified maturities, such as credit card loans, ascertain the effective maturities or repricing dates for those loans and assess the potential exposure for the bank.

2.   If the bank has substantial volumes of medium- or longer-term fixed rate loans, assess how appreciation or depreciation of these loans could affect the bank's capital.

3.   If the bank has substantial volumes of adjustable-rate mortgage products and other loans with explicit caps, evaluate the effect of those caps on the bank's future earnings and at what level of interest rates those caps would come into effect.

4.   Assess how a substantial increase in interest rates would affect the credit performance of the bank's loan portfolio.

5.   If the bank incorporates and enforces prepayment penalties on medium- or longer-term fixed rate loans, assess the effect of penalties on optionality of these loans.

Investment Portfolios

1.   Review the investment trial balance and list of investment purchases to determine the nature and maturity/repricing composition of the bank's investment portfolio.

2.   If the bank has substantial volumes of medium- or longer-term fixed rate investments, determine the actual and potential appreciation or depreciation of such investments. Assess how appreciation or depreciation could affect the bank's earnings and capital.

3.   If the bank has substantial volumes of investments with explicit or embedded options, evaluate the effect of those options on the bank's future earnings and at what level of interest rates those options might be exercised.

Deposit Accounts

1.   Assess how the bank's deposits might react in different rate environments. Consider management's assumptions for:

Implicit or explicit floors or ceilings on deposit rates.
Rate sensitivity of the bank's depositor base and deposit products.

2.   Determine the reasonableness of the bank's assumptions about the effective maturity of the bank's deposits and evaluate to what extent the bank's deposit base could offset interest rate risk.

3.   Analyze trends in deposit accounts. Consider:

- Stability of offering rates.
- Increasing or declining balances.
- Large depositor concentrations.
- Seasonal and cyclical variations in deposit balances.

Off-Balance Sheet Derivatives

Coordinate the following steps with the examiner assigned to review derivatives activities, as applicable.

1.   Determine whether management uses off-balance sheet derivative interest rate contracts to manage its interest rate risk exposure. Distinguish between the following activities:

- Risk reduction activities that use derivatives to reduce the volatility of earnings or to stabilize the economic value in a particular asset, liability, or business.
- Positioning activities that use derivatives as investment substitutes or specifically to alter the institution's overall interest rate risk profile.

2.   Assess the impact of off-balance sheet derivatives on the bank's interest rate risk profile given management's stated intent for their use.

Other Sources of Interest Rate Risk

1.   If the bank has other sources of interest rate risk, such as mortgage servicing, credit card servicing, or other loan servicing assets, determine the sensitivity of these other sources to changes in interest rates and the potential impact on earnings and capital.

Quality of Risk Management

Conclusion: The quality of risk management is (strong, satisfactory, weak).

Policy

Conclusion: The bank's policies for controlling the nature and amount of interest rate risk are (satisfactory/unsatisfactory).

Objective: To determine the adequacy of policies regarding interest rate risk.

1.   Determine if the board has approved an interest rate risk policy that:

- Establishes a risk management process for identifying, measuring, monitoring, and controlling risk.
- Establishes risk tolerances, risk limits, and responsibility for managing risk.
- Is appropriate for the nature and complexity of the bank's interest rate risk exposure.
- Is periodically reassessed in light of changes in market conditions and bank activities.

2.   Review the bank's derivatives activities to determine whether such activities are consistent with the board's interest rate risk strategies and policies. If so, determine whether the use of such derivatives allows the bank to achieve those strategies effectively.

Processes

Conclusion: Management and the board (have/have not) implemented effective processes to manage interest rate risk.

Objective: To evaluate the effectiveness of the bank's identification of its interest rate risk exposure.

1.   Assess the bank's strategies for managing interest rate risk and the instruments and portfolios used to manage the risk.

2.   Determine whether the bank's management information systems (MIS) provide sufficient historical, trend, and customer information to help bank personnel formulate and evaluate assumptions regarding customer behavior. Consider, where material, if information is available to analyze:

- Loan or mortgage-backed security prepayments.
- Early deposit withdrawals.
- Spreads between administered rate products, such as prime-based loans and nonmaturity deposit accounts, and market rates of interest.

3.   Determine whether the bank's MIS provides adequate and timely information for assessing the interest rate risk exposure in the bank's current on- and off-balance sheet positions. Determine whether information is available for all the bank's material portfolios, lines of business, and operating units.

Considerations
- Current outstanding balances, rates/coupons, and repricing indices.
- Contractual maturities or repricing dates.
- Contractual caps or floors on interest rates.
- Scheduled amortizations and repayments.
- Introductory "teaser" rates.

4.   Determine whether the bank's method of aggregating data is sufficient for analysis purposes given the nature

---

and scope of the bank's interest rate risk exposure(s).

Considerations
- If a bank has significant holdings of fixed-rate residential mortgage-related products, determine if coupon data is captured in sufficient detail to allow the bank to reasonably assess its prepayment and extension risks.
- If a bank has significant holdings of adjustable-rate residential mortgage-related products, determine whether:
  - Data on periodic and lifetime caps is captured in sufficient detail to permit adequate analysis.
  - The effect of teaser rates as well as the type of rate indices used (current versus lagging) has been factored into the bank's risk measurement system.
  - Data permits the bank to monitor the prepayment, default, and extension risks of the products.

Loan Portfolios

1. If the bank has substantial volumes of loans with unspecified maturities, such as credit card loans, discuss with management the assumptions and methods used to assess the effective maturities or repricing dates for those loans.

2. If the bank has substantial volumes of medium- or longer-term fixed rate loans, determine whether and how management monitors and evaluates the actual or potential appreciation or depreciation in those portfolios. Also determine whether management assesses how appreciation or depreciation could affect the bank's earnings and capital. The potential appreciation or depreciation should be calculated over a range of potential interest rate movements. The rate changes should include at least a 200 basis point change in rates over one year as well as changes in the shape and level of the yield curve.

3. If the bank has substantial volumes of mortgage products and other loans with explicit caps, determine whether and how management monitors and evaluates the effect of those caps on the bank's future earnings and at what level of interest rates those caps would come into effect.

4. Determine whether management periodically assesses how a substantial increase in interest rates may affect the credit performance of its loan portfolio.

5. Determine whether management incorporates and enforces prepayment penalties on medium- or longer-term fixed rate loans.

Investment Portfolios

1. Discuss with management their investment strategies to manage interest rate risk. Determine whether the bank's classification and accounting treatment for its investment holdings are appropriate given management's strategies and actions.

2. If the bank has substantial volumes of medium- or longer-term fixed rate investments, determine whether and how management evaluates and monitors the actual and potential appreciation or depreciation of such investments. Also determine whether management assesses how appreciation or depreciation could affect the bank's earnings and capital. The potential appreciation or depreciation should be calculated over a range of potential interest rate movements. The rate changes should include at least a 200 basis point change in rates over one year as well as changes in the shape and level of the yield curve.

Deposit Accounts

1. Determine whether management performs a sensitivity analysis on deposit assumptions. In particular,

determine whether management analyzes how its interest rate exposure may change if those assumptions change or prove to be incorrect and what action, if any, would be taken.

2.   Determine whether management has analyzed the bank's deposit base.

Considerations
- Whether management has estimated how the bank's deposits will react in different rate environments.
- Whether the analysis considered the bank's pricing policy.
- How competitors' actions may affect the bank's pricing policy.

Off-Balance Sheet Derivatives

1.   Determine whether management obtains or develops reliable and independent estimates for the value and value sensitivity of its off-balance sheet derivatives. The estimates should be calculated over a range of potential interest rate movements. The rate changes should include at least a 200 basis point change in rates over one year, as well as changes in the shape and level of the yield curve.

Other Sources of Interest Rate Risk

1.   Determine whether management understands and effectively measures other sources of interest rate risk, such as mortgage servicing, credit card servicing, or other loan servicing assets.

Objective: To determine if the bank's interest rate risk measurement systems are appropriate for the nature and complexity of its activities.

1.   Determine the type of interest rate risk measurement systems used by the bank and evaluate the adequacy of those systems. Do they:

- Identify and measure the bank's major sources of interest rate risk exposure?
- Provide estimates of the bank's exposures in a timely and comprehensive manner?
- Capture and adequately evaluate assets and liabilities with embedded options?
- Measure the bank's earnings-at-risk from changes in interest rates?
- Identify and measure significant medium- and long-term positions?
- Measure the bank's capital at risk from changes in the economic value of balance sheet and off-balance sheet items?
- Handle the risk characteristics of the bank's business lines and products?

2.   Identify the interest rate scenarios the bank uses to measure its potential interest rate risk exposures. Assess the adequacy of such rate scenarios. Do they:

- Cover a reasonable range of potential interest rate movements in light of historical rate movements?
- Allow the bank to consider the impact of at least a 200 basis point interest rate change over a one-year time horizon?
- Reasonably anticipate holding periods or the time it may take to implement risk-mitigating actions given the bank's strategies, activities, market access, and management abilities?
- Sufficiently capture the potential risks arising from option-related positions?

3.   Discuss with management the key assumptions underlying the bank's risk measurement models. Determine if:

- Assumptions are periodically reviewed for reasonableness.

- Major assumptions are documented and their sensitivity tested, and results communicated to senior management and the board at least annually.
- Assumptions are reasonable in light of the bank's product mix, business strategy, historical experience, and competitive market.
- Cash flow assumptions for products with option features are reasonable and consistent with the interest rate scenario that is being evaluated.

4. Determine whether management performs a sensitivity analysis on deposit assumptions. In particular, determine whether management analyzes how its interest rate exposure may change if those assumptions change or prove to be incorrect and what action, if any, would be taken.

The next set of procedures is specific to the type of measurement model used by the bank. Select only those procedures that are appropriate.

Gap Reports

1. If the bank uses gap (repricing) reports, do the reports:

- Include all assets, liabilities, and relevant off-balance sheet items? If certain items are not included, determine why.
- Reflect reasonable assumptions for placing balance sheet items into various maturity categories or time bands?
- Include a sufficient number of time bands to permit effective monitoring of both short- and long-term exposures? If not, require additional breakdowns because the volume and proportion of assets and liabilities grouped into a single category is too aggregated.
- Allow management to reasonably estimate the maturities of assets and liabilities with noncontractual repricing dates (i.e., for demand deposits, savings, and credit cards)?
- Allow bank management to consider seasonal fluctuations, historic volume trends, and customer behavior patterns?
- Allow management to consider embedded options that might be exercised by a customer? (Banks should use a different gap report for each interest rate scenario. The embedded options may include deposit withdrawals, mortgage prepayments, and caps and floors on floating rate instruments.)

Simulation Models (Earnings or Economic)

1. If the bank uses a simulation model, determine:

- Whether an outside vendor designed the model or whether it was developed internally.
- The role and use of the simulation model in the bank's interest rate risk management operations. Determine whether the model is the primary indicator of existing interest rate risk or whether it is also used to test the impact of future or alternative strategies.
- Whether management evaluates simulation model output against actual results in order to discern any weaknesses in the model.

2. Review the capabilities of the model to determine whether the model:

- Identifies and quantifies exposure to net income or economic value.
- Allows the bank to measure its interest rate risk from various sources and over different time frames.
- Allows the bank to conduct sensitivity tests of key assumptions including:
    - Yield curve, spread, and pricing relationships.
    - Loan and investment prepayments.
    - Nonmaturity deposit behavior.

3. Review the data requirements and input to the model to determine whether:

    - Data needed for the model are available and complete.
    - The model allows the bank to incorporate data reflecting:
        - Current and new business.
        - Mergers and acquisitions.
        - Changes in spread and yield curve relationships.
        - Embedded and explicit options.
        - Off-balance sheet derivative instruments.
    - Model assumptions regarding future volume and growth are reasonable and consistent with management's goals and with the rate scenarios used within the model.
    - Data are accurately aggregated for all significant sources throughout the bank (or bank holding company).
    - Data are reconciled.

4. Review a description of the model's calculation method to determine how:

    - Cash flow estimates are derived for instruments with indeterminate maturities, such as credit cards, nonmaturity deposits, or instruments with embedded options.
    - Balance sheet forecasts are derived and if the structure is consistent with the bank's assumptions for growth.

5. If the model focuses solely on the effect of interest rate risk on net income, determine whether the bank has significant medium- or long-term exposures. If so, what systems are used to monitor and control the risk from these exposures.

6. If the model measures the effect of interest rate risk on economic value, determine:

    - Whether the model measures the bank's economic value in the current interest rate environment to identify "embedded losses" that the bank has already incurred, as well as the bank's exposure to prospective interest rate changes.
    - Types and sources of discount rates used to derive net present values.
    - Whether the model results are clearly communicated to senior management. This generally requires reporting the ranges of economic value that correspond to a range of interest rates. The range of rate changes should include at least a 200 basis point change in rates over one year as well as changes in the shape and level of the yield curve.

Objective: To assess the quality of controls for interest rate risk.

1. Determine the types of risk limits used to control interest rate risk and ascertain their effectiveness. Do the limits address:

    - Range of possible interest rate changes?
    - Potential impact of interest changes on both earnings and economic value of equity?

2. Determine whether the bank has established a level of earnings it is willing to risk given an adverse movement in interest rates. If bank management uses gap ratios to limit interest rate risk, determine whether these limits are converted to an earnings-at-risk limit.

3. Determine whether management establishes limits for longer-term exposures or repricing (gap) imbalances.

Examples are limits on:

- Positions for individual portfolios.
- Size of medium- and longer-term gaps.
- Sensitivity of the bank's economic value of equity.

4.   Determine whether the bank operates within its established limits and risk tolerances. Determine how limit exceptions are monitored, reported to management, and approved.

5.   Determine whether the bank's risk limits are prudent in view of the bank's financial condition, the quality of its risk management practices and managerial expertise, and its capital base.

6.   Determine whether there are sufficient controls in place to monitor and control the taking of interest rate positions through the bank's loan activities. Discuss with management their policies regarding loan pricing and maturities and the development of new loan products or structures.

7.   Determine whether separation of duties and lines of responsibility and authority are enforced.

8. Determine whether the internal controls are appropriate for the type and level of interest rate risk of the bank.

Personnel

Conclusion: The board and management personnel (do/do not) possess the required skills and knowledge to effectively manage interest rate risk.

Objective: To evaluate the capabilities of key personnel.

1.   Determine whether management is technically qualified and capable of properly managing the interest rate risk exposure of the bank. Review:

- Brief biographies of managers of units responsible for interest rate risk management.
- Job descriptions for key positions.

2.   Review staffing levels, educational background, and work experience of the staff. Determine whether the bank has sufficient and qualified staff.

3.   Review compensation plans, including incentive components, for staff that manage the bank's interest rate risk exposure. Determine if the plans:

- Are designed to recruit, develop, and retain appropriate talent.
- Encourage employees to take risk that is incompatible with the bank's risk appetite or prevailing rules or regulations.
- Are consistent with the long-term strategic goals of the bank.
- Include compliance with bank policies, laws, and regulations.
- Consider performance relative to the bank's stated goals.
- Consider competitors' compensation packages for similar responsibilities and performance.
- Consider individual overall performance.

4.   Determine whether the board holds management accountable for performance. Consider:

- Consistency of performance against strategic and financial objectives over time.
- Internal/external audit and regulatory examination results.

- Level of compliance with policies and procedures.

Controls

Conclusion: Management and the board have implemented (effective/ineffective) control systems.

Objective: To assess the quality of risk monitoring and reporting of interest rate risk.

1. Determine whether the measurement systems provide reports in a format that senior management and the board can readily understand, enabling them to make timely decisions and monitor compliance with stated objectives and risk limits.

2. Determine whether the bank has an effective system for monitoring its interest rate risk exposures and reporting on those exposures to senior management and the board. Do the reporting systems allow senior management and the board to:

   - Evaluate the level and trends of the bank's (or, if a part of a multibank holding company, the company's) aggregate interest rate risk exposure?
   - Evaluate the sensitivity of key assumptions?
   - Evaluate the trade-offs between risk levels and performance?
   - Verify compliance with the board's established risk tolerance levels?
   - Determine whether the bank holds sufficient capital for the level of risk being taken?

3. Determine whether timely reports to senior management and the board are provided at least quarterly.

Objective: To assess the controls for interest rate risk model integrity.

1. Determine whether the bank periodically conducts integrity checks of its risk measurement systems by comparing model output and exposure estimates against actual results in order to reveal any material weaknesses in the models or assumptions.

2. If the bank uses a model designed by an outside vendor, determine whether model integrity is maintained. Consider whether:

   - Models are upgraded and kept current.
   - Bank staff members understand the key methods used by the model to generate exposure estimates.
   - Bank staff members have received sufficient training and have sufficient documentation on the model to ensure that bank staff can successfully use and interpret model results.
   - Management has assessed whether the vendor can and will continue to provide ongoing support and documentation of the model and its methods.

3. If the bank uses a model developed internally, determine whether model integrity is maintained. Consider whether:

   - Sufficient documentation for the model's methods, operating code, and data sources exist so that the model's operation is not solely dependent on one or two key employees.
   - Model is kept current.
   - A source independent of the persons or units that developed and maintain the model has tested and validated the model's calculations and methods.

Objective: To assess the adequacy of the review/audit of the risk management process.

1.   Review the scope of the review/audit of the interest rate risk management process to determine its completeness and whether the review/audit is sufficiently independent and frequent. At a minimum, the audit should include the following checks:

- Periodic appraisal of the adequacy of the interest rate risk management process, including its limits and controls.
- Appropriateness of the bank's risk measurement system(s) given the nature, scope, and complexity of its activities.
- Independent verification of the accuracy of interest rate risk measurement systems (including GAP reports, earnings, and economic value simulation models).
- Reasonableness of interest rate scenarios and assumptions used in the risk measurement systems.
- Independent verification of the accuracy and completeness of the data used in the risk measurement systems.

2.   Determine if individuals conducting the review/audit have the appropriate background to conduct such a review.

3.   Determine whether audit findings, and management responses to those findings, are fully documented and tracked for adequate follow up.

4.   Determine whether management gives identified material weaknesses appropriate and timely attention.

5.   Determine whether management's actions taken in response to material weaknesses have been verified and reviewed by senior management and the board.

6.   Determine whether the board and senior management have established clear lines of authority and responsibility for monitoring compliance with policies, procedures, and limits.

Conclusion

Objective: To prepare written conclusion comments and communicate findings to management. Review findings with the EIC prior to discussion with management.

1. Based on the quantity of interest rate risk and quality of interest rate risk management, evaluate the adequacy of the bank's capital. Consider:

    *   Whether there is significant depreciation in the bank's current balance sheet positions from past interest rate movements.
    *   Potential adverse exposure to earnings and capital from future interest rate movements.
    *   Adequacy and effectiveness of the bank's interest rate risk management and measurement processes, including its ability to identify adverse risk exposures in a timely manner and to take prompt remedial action.
    *   Strength and stability of the bank's earnings stream.

2. Determine the CAMELS component rating for sensitivity to market risk. Consider:

    *   Management's ability to identify, monitor and control interest rate risk.
    *   Bank size.
    *   Nature and complexity of the bank's activities.
    *   Adequacy of the bank's capital and earnings in relation to its level of interest rate risk exposure.

3. Determine the impact on the aggregate and direction of risk assessments for any applicable risks identified by performing the above procedures. Examiners should refer to guidance provided under the OCC's large and community bank risk assessment programs.

    *   Risk Categories: Compliance, Credit, Foreign Currency Translation, Interest Rate, Liquidity, Price, Reputation, Strategic, Transaction
    *   Risk Conclusions: High, Moderate, or Low
    *   Risk Direction: Increasing, Stable, or Decreasing

For banks with an S component rating of 1 or 2:

1. Provide the EIC with brief conclusions regarding:

    *   Nature and complexity of interest rate exposure.
    *   Sensitivity of the bank's earnings and economic value of its capital to adverse changes in interest rates.
    *   Ability of management to identify, measure, monitor, and control the interest rate risk exposure given the bank's size, complexity, and risk profile.

2. Determine, in consultation with the EIC, if the risks identified are significant enough to merit bringing them to the board's attention in the report of examination. If so, prepare items for inclusion under the heading Matters Requiring Board Attention. MRBA should cover practices that deviate from sound fundamental principles and are likely to result in financial deterioration if not addressed. MRBA should discuss:

    *   Causative factors contributing to the problem.
    *   Consequences of inaction.
    *   Management's commitment for corrective action.
    *   Time frames and person(s) responsible for corrective action.

3. Discuss findings with management including conclusions regarding interest rate risk exposure. The

discussion should include:

- Any potential sources of interest rate risk that the bank has not adequately identified or included in its interest rate risk management process.
- Adequacy of the bank's capital for the level of interest rate risk assumed.

4. As appropriate, prepare a brief interest rate risk comment for inclusion in the report of examination. The comment should include:

- Major sources of the bank's interest rate risk.
- Level of interest rate risk assumed by the bank.
- Quality of the bank's interest rate risk management process.
- Adequacy of the bank's capital.
- Deficiencies noted in the bank's interest rate risk management process.
- Actions needed to improve the bank's identification, measurement, monitoring, and control of its interest rate risk.

5. Prepare a memorandum or update the work program with any information which will facilitate future examinations.

6. Update the OCC database and any applicable report of examination schedules or tables.

7. Organize and reference working papers in accordance with OCC guidance.

For banks with an S component rating of 3 or worse:

1. Provide a detailed conclusion comment to the EIC. Discuss:

- Adverse effect of interest rate changes on the bank's earnings and economic value of its capital.
- Adequacy of capital for the level of risk assumed by the bank.
- Weaknesses identified in the bank's interest rate risk management process including:
  - Effectiveness of board and senior management oversight.
  - Bank's ability to identify sources of interest rate risk.
  - Bank's ability to measure interest rate risk and the appropriateness or effectiveness of the interest rate risk measurement system.
  - Completeness and timeliness of the interest rate risk reports provided to the board and senior management.
  - Effectiveness of the interest rate risk limits established by the bank to control the risk.

2. Assess whether management is able to correct the bank's fundamental problems. Consider the following:

- Does the bank have staff with the necessary skills and experience to effectively manage its interest rate risk exposure?
- If not, are senior management and the board willing to hire staff with the appropriate skills?
- In the current economic environment, can the bank reduce its interest rate risk exposure without jeopardizing its safety and soundness?
- Does the bank have access to additional capital to withstand losses from interest rate risk?

3. Develop, in consultation with the EIC, a strategy to address the bank's weaknesses and discuss the strategy with the appropriate supervisory office or manager. Consider:

- Level of capital at the bank.
- Knowledge and skills of existing staff and likelihood of the bank hiring/attracting more qualified staff.
- Board and senior management's understanding of interest rate risk.
- Business strategy of the bank.

4. Determine in consultation with the EIC, if the risks identified are significant enough to merit bringing them to the board's attention in the report of examination. If so, prepare items for inclusion under the heading Matters Requiring Board Attention. MRBA should cover practices that deviate from sound fundamental principles and are likely to result in financial deterioration if not addressed. MRBA should discuss:

- Causative factors contributing to the problem.
- Consequences of inaction.
- Management's commitment for corrective action.
- The time frame and person(s) responsible for corrective action.

5. Discuss findings with management including conclusions regarding interest rate risk exposure. Discussion should include:

- Any potential sources of interest rate risk that the bank has not adequately identified or included in its interest rate risk management process.
- The adequacy of the bank's capital for the level of interest rate risk assumed.

6. Prepare an interest rate risk comment for inclusion in the report of examination. The comment should include:

- Major sources of the bank's interest rate risk.
- Level of interest rate risk assumed by the bank.
- Quality of the bank's interest rate risk management process.
- Adequacy of the bank's capital.
- Deficiencies noted in the bank's interest rate risk management process.
- Actions needed to improve the bank's identification, measurement, monitoring, and control of its interest rate risk.

7. Prepare a memorandum or update the work program with any information which will facilitate future examinations.

8. Update the OCC database and any applicable report of examination schedules or tables.

9. Organize and reference working papers in accordance with OCC guidance.

Interest Rate Risk

Appendix A

Joint Agency Policy Statement
on Interest Rate Risk

Purpose

This joint agency policy statement ("statement") provides guidance to banks on prudent interest rate risk management principles. The three federal banking agencies – the Board of Governors of the Federal Reserve System, the Federal Deposit Insurance Corporation, and the Office of the Comptroller of the Currency ("agencies") – believe that effective interest rate risk management is an essential component of safe and sound banking practices. The agencies are issuing this statement to provide guidance to banks on this subject and to assist bankers and examiners in evaluating the adequacy of a bank's management of interest rate risk.[1]

This statement applies to all federally insured commercial and FDIC supervised savings banks ["banks"]. Because market conditions, bank structures, and bank activities vary, each bank needs to develop its own interest rate risk management program tailored to its needs and circumstances. Nonetheless, there are certain elements that are fundamental to sound interest rate risk management, including appropriate board and senior management oversight and a comprehensive risk management process that effectively identifies, measures, monitors and controls risk. This statement describes prudent principles and practices for each of these elements.

The adequacy and effectiveness of a bank's interest rate risk management process and the level of its interest rate exposure are critical factors in the agencies' evaluation of the bank's capital adequacy. A bank with material weaknesses in its risk management process or high levels of exposure relative to its capital will be directed by the agencies to take corrective action. Such actions will include recommendations or directives to raise additional capital, strengthen management expertise, improve management information and measurement systems, reduce levels of exposure, or some combination thereof, depending on the facts and circumstances of the individual institution.

When evaluating the applicability of specific guidelines provided in this statement and the level of capital needed for interest rate risk, bank management and examiners should consider factors such as the size of the bank, the nature and complexity of its activities, and the adequacy of its capital and earnings in relation to the bank's overall risk profile.

Background

Interest rate risk is the exposure of a bank's financial condition to adverse movements in interest rates. It results from differences in the maturity or timing of coupon adjustments of bank assets, liabilities and off-balance-sheet instruments (repricing or maturity-mismatch risk); from changes in the slope of the yield curve (yield curve risk); from imperfect correlations in the adjustment of rates earned and paid on different instruments with otherwise similar repricing characteristics (basis risk – e.g., three-month Treasury bill versus three-month Libor); and from interest-rate-related options embedded in bank products (option risk).

---

[1] The focus of this statement is on the interest rate risk found in banks nontrading activities. Each agency has separate guidance regarding the prudent risk management of trading activities.

Changes in interest rates affect a bank's earnings by changing its net interest income and the level of other interest sensitive income and operating expenses. Changes in interest rates also affect the underlying economic value[1] of the bank's assets, liabilities, and off-balance-sheet instruments because the present value of future cash flows and in some cases, the cash flows themselves, change when interest rates change. The combined effects of the changes in these present values reflect the change in the bank's underlying economic value.

As financial intermediaries banks accept and manage interest rate risk as an inherent part of their business. Although banks have always had to manage interest rate risk, changes in the competitive environment in which banks operate and in the products and services they offer have increased the importance of prudently managing this risk. This guidance is intended to highlight the key elements of prudent interest rate risk management. The agencies expect that in implementing this guidance, bank boards of directors and senior managements will provide effective oversight and ensure that risks are adequately identified, measured, monitored and controlled.

Board and Senior Management Oversight

Effective board and senior management oversight of a bank's interest rate risk activities is the cornerstone of a sound risk management process. The board and senior management are responsible for understanding the nature and level of interest rate risk being taken by the bank and how that risk fits within the overall business strategies of the bank. They are also responsible for ensuring that the formality and sophistication of the risk management process is appropriate for the overall level of risk. Effective risk management requires an informed board, capable management and appropriate staffing.

For its part, a bank's board of directors has two broad responsibilities:

- To establish and guide the bank's tolerance for interest rate risk, including approving relevant risk limits and other key policies, identifying lines of authority and responsibility for managing risk, and ensuring adequate resources are devoted to interest rate risk management.

- To monitor the bank's overall interest rate risk profile and ensure that the level of interest rate risk is maintained at prudent levels.

Senior management is responsible for ensuring that interest rate risk is managed for both the long range and day to day. In managing the bank's activities, senior management should:

- Develop and implement policies and procedures that translate the board's goals, objectives, and risk limits into operating standards that are well understood by bank personnel and that are consistent with the board's intent.

- Ensure adherence to the lines of authority and responsibility that the board has approved for measuring, managing, and reporting interest rate risk exposures.

- Oversee the implementation and maintenance of management information and other systems that identify, measure, monitor, and control the bank's interest rate risk.

- Establish internal controls over the interest rate risk management process.

Risk Management Process

Effective control of interest rate risk requires a comprehensive risk management process that includes the following elements:

- Policies and procedures designed to control the nature and amount of interest rate risk the bank takes including those that specify risk limits and define lines of responsibilities and authority for managing risk.

- A system for identifying and measuring interest rate risk.

- A system for monitoring and reporting risk exposures.

- A system of internal controls, review, and audit to ensure the integrity of the overall risk management process.

The formality and sophistication of these elements may vary significantly among institutions, depending on the level of the bank's risk and the complexity of its holdings and activities. Banks with noncomplex activities and relatively short-term

---

[1] The economic value of an instrument represents an assessment of the present value of the expected net future cash flows of the instrument, discounted to reflect market rates. A bank's economic value of equity (EVE) represents the present value of the expected cash flows on assets minus the present value of the expected cash flows on liabilities, plus or minus the present value of the expected cash flows on off-balance-sheet instruments.

balance sheet structures presenting relatively low risk levels and whose senior managers are actively involved in the details of day-to-day operations may be able to rely on a relatively basic and less formal interest rate risk management process, provided their procedures for managing and controlling risks are communicated clearly and are well understood by all relevant parties.

More complex organizations and those with higher interest rate risk exposures or holdings of complex instruments with significant interest rate-related option characteristics may require more elaborate and formal interest rate risk management processes. Risk management processes for these banks should address the institution's broader and typically more complex range of financial activities and provide senior managers with the information they need to monitor and direct day-to-day activities. Moreover, the more complex interest rate risk management processes employed at these institutions require adequate internal controls that include internal and/or external audits or other appropriate oversight mechanisms to ensure the integrity of the information used by the board and senior management in overseeing compliance with policies and limits. Those individuals involved in the risk management process (or risk management units) in these banks must be sufficiently independent of the business lines to ensure adequate separation of duties and to avoid conflicts of interest.

Risk Controls and Limits

The board and senior management should ensure that the structure of the bank's business and the level of interest rate risk it assumes are effectively managed and that appropriate policies and practices are established to control and limit risks. This includes delineating clear lines of responsibility and authority for the following areas:

- Identifying the potential interest rate risk arising from existing or new products or activities;
- Establishing and maintaining an interest rate risk measurement system;
- Formulating and executing strategies to manage interest rate risk exposures; and
- Authorizing policy exceptions.

In some institutions the board and senior management may rely on a committee of senior managers to manage this process. An institution should also have policies for identifying the types of instruments and activities that the bank may use to manage its interest rate risk exposure. Such policies should clearly identify permissible instruments, either specifically or by their characteristics, and should also describe the purposes or objectives for which they may be used. As appropriate to the size and complexity of the bank, the policies should also help delineate procedures for acquiring specific instruments, managing portfolios, and controlling the bank's aggregate interest rate risk exposure.

Policies that establish appropriate risk limits that reflect the board's risk tolerance are an important part of an institution's risk management process and control structure. At a minimum these limits should be board approved and ensure that the institution's interest rate exposure will not lead to an unsafe and unsound condition. Senior management should maintain a bank's exposure within the board-approved limits. Limit controls should ensure that positions that exceed certain predetermined levels receive prompt management attention. An appropriate limit system should permit management to control interest rate risk exposures, initiate discussion about opportunities and risk, and monitor actual risk taking against predetermined risk tolerances.

A bank's limits should be consistent with the bank's overall approach to measuring interest rate risk and should be based on capital levels, earnings, performance, and the risk tolerance of the institution. The limits should be appropriate to the size, complexity and capital adequacy of the institution and address the potential impact of changes in market interest rates on both reported earnings and the bank's economic value of equity (EVE). From an earnings perspective a bank should explore limits on net income as well as net interest income in order to fully assess the contribution of noninterest income to the interest rate risk exposure of the bank. Such limits usually specify acceptable levels of earnings volatility under specified interest rate scenarios. A bank's EVE limits should reflect the size and complexity of its underlying positions. For banks with few holdings of complex instruments and low risk profiles, simple limits on permissible holdings or allowable repricing mismatches in intermediate- and long-term instruments may be adequate. At more complex institutions, more extensive limit structures may be necessary. Banks that have significant intermediate- and long-term mismatches or complex options positions should have limits in place that quantify and constrain the potential changes in economic value or capital of the bank that could arise from those positions.

Identification and Measurement

Accurate and timely identification and measurement of interest rate risk are necessary for proper risk management and control. The type of measurement system that a bank requires to operate prudently depends upon the nature and mix of its business lines and the interest rate risk characteristics of its activities. The bank's measurement system(s) should enable management to recognize and identify risks arising from the bank's existing activities and from new business initiatives. It should also facilitate accurate and timely measurement of its current and potential interest rate risk exposure.

The agencies believe that a well-managed bank will consider both earnings and economic perspectives when assessing the full scope of its interest rate risk exposure. The impact on earnings is important because reduced earnings or outright losses can adversely affect a bank's liquidity and capital adequacy. Evaluating the possibility of an adverse change in a bank's economic value of equity is also useful, since it can signal future earnings and capital problems. Changes in economic value can also affect the liquidity of bank assets, because the cost of selling depreciated assets to meet liquidity needs may be prohibitive.

Since the value of instruments with intermediate and long maturities or embedded options is especially sensitive to interest rate changes, banks with significant holdings of these instruments should be able to assess the potential long-term impact of changes in interest rates on the value of these positions and the future performance of the bank.

Measurement systems for evaluating the effect of rates on earnings may focus on either net interest income or net income. Institutions with significant noninterest income that is sensitive to changing rates should focus special attention on net income. Measurement systems used to assess the effect of changes in interest rates on reported earnings range from simple maturity gap reports to more sophisticated income simulation models. Measurement approaches for evaluating the potential effect on economic value of an institution may, depending on the size and complexity of the institution, range from basic position reports on holdings of intermediate, long-term, and/or complex instruments to simple mismatch weighting techniques to formal static or dynamic cash flow valuation models.

Regardless of the type and level of complexity of the measurement system used, bank management should ensure the adequacy and completeness of the system. Because the quality and reliability of the measurement system is largely dependent upon the quality of the data and various assumptions used in the model, management should give particular attention to these items.

The measurement system should include all material interest rate positions of the bank and consider all relevant repricing and maturity data. Such information will generally include: (i) current balance and contractual rate of interest associated with the instruments and portfolios, (ii) principal payments, interest reset dates, maturities, and (iii) the rate index used for repricing and contractual interest rate ceilings or floors for adjustable rate items. The system should also have well-documented assumptions and techniques.

Bank management should ensure that risk is measured over a probable range of potential interest rate changes, including meaningful stress situations. In developing appropriate rate scenarios, bank management should consider a variety of factors such as the shape and level of the current term structure of interest rates and historical rate movements. The scenarios used should incorporate a sufficiently wide change in market interest rates (e.g., plus or minus 200 basis points over a one-year horizon) and include immediate or gradual changes in market interest rates as well as changes in the shape of the yield curve in order to capture the material effects of any explicit or embedded options.

Assumptions about customer behavior and new business activity should be reasonable and consistent with each rate scenario that is evaluated. In particular, as part of its measurement process, bank management should consider how the maturity, repricing and cash flows of instruments with embedded options may change under various scenarios. Such instruments would include loans that can be prepaid without penalty prior to maturity or have limits on the coupon adjustments, and deposits with unspecified maturities or rights of early withdrawal.

Monitoring and Reporting Exposures

Institutions should also establish an adequate system for monitoring and reporting risk exposures. A bank's senior management and its board or a board committee should receive reports on the bank's interest risk profile at least quarterly. More frequent reporting may be appropriate depending on the bank's level of risk and the potential that the level of risk could change significantly. These reports should allow senior management and the board or committee to:

- Evaluate the level and trends of the bank's aggregated interest rate risk exposure.

- Evaluate the sensitivity and reasonableness of key assumptions C such as those dealing with changes in the shape of the yield curve or in the pace of anticipated loan prepayments or deposit withdrawals.

- Verify compliance with the board's established risk tolerance levels and limits and identify any policy exceptions.

- Determine whether the bank holds sufficient capital for the level of interest rate risk being taken.

The reports provided to the board and senior management should be clear, concise, and timely and provide the information needed for making decisions.

Internal Control, Review, and Audit of the Risk Management Process

A bank's internal control structure is critical to the safe and sound functioning of the organization generally, and to its interest rate risk management process in particular. Establishing and maintaining an effective system of controls, including the enforcement of official lines of authority and the appropriate separation of duties, are two of management's more important responsibilities. Individuals responsible for evaluating risk monitoring and control procedures should be independent of the function they are assigned to review.

Effective control of the interest rate risk management process includes independent review and, where appropriate, internal and external audit. The bank should conduct periodic reviews of its risk management process to ensure its integrity, accuracy, and reasonableness. Items that should be reviewed and validated include:

- The adequacy of, and personnel's compliance with, the bank's internal control system.

- The appropriateness of the bank's risk measurement system given the nature, scope, and complexity of its activities.

- The accuracy and completeness of the data inputs into the bank's risk measurement system.

- The reasonableness and validity of scenarios used in the risk measurement system.

- The validity of the risk measurement calculations. The validity of the calculations is often tested by comparing actual versus forecasted results.

The scope and formality of the review and validation will depend on the size and complexity of the bank. At large banks, internal and external auditors may have their own models against which the bank's model is tested. Banks with complex risk measurement systems should have their models or calculations validated by an independent source C either an internal risk control unit of the bank or by outside auditors or consultants.

The findings of this review should be reported to the board annually. The report should provide a brief summary of the bank's interest rate risk measurement techniques and management practices. It also should identify major critical assumptions used in the risk measurement process, discuss the process used to derive those assumptions and provide an assessment of the impact of those assumptions on the bank's measured exposure.

Interest Rate Risk

Appendix B

Earnings versus Economic Perspectives --
A Numerical Example

A bank's interest rate risk should not be viewed solely in terms of its effects on either economic value or earnings. These two perspectives are complementary, and both are necessary to capture interest rate risk comprehensively.

The economic perspective focuses on the value of the bank in today's interest rate environment and the sensitivity of that value to changes in interest rates. It also captures future exposure by evaluating the impact of potential rate changes on market values of all assets, liabilities, and off-balance-sheet contracts.

The earnings perspective, which captures the *timing* of income effects, helps risk managers determine what action to take to offset or hedge the exposure. In the example in this appendix, the accounting perspective indicates that earnings problems will not develop until the second year in which the assets and liabilities are on the bank's balance sheet.

The bank in the example is exposed to interest rate risk arising from the repricing gap between a four-year asset and a one-year liability. Both instruments are accounted for on an historic cost basis.

Table 1 illustrates the expected annual income and cash flows for this bank, assuming that interest rates remain at their current levels. The example uses the following simplifying assumptions:

- The bank has equity capital of $200 million.
- The bank has a four-year note carrying an 8 percent coupon. The face amount is $1.2 million and the current market value is par. The note pays interest annually.
- The bank funds the note with a one-year certificate of deposit with a face amount of $1 million. The current rate on the CD is 6 percent and interest is paid annually.
- The bank pays all of its income to shareholders as dividends and pays no taxes. It has no other income or operating expenses.
- At the end of the fourth year, the bank plans to liquidate and distribute any residual equity to shareholders.

Under this scenario, the bank expects to earn $36,000 each year on the spread between its asset and liability. Shareholders would receive $36,000 in dividends in each year. At the end of the fourth year, the bank receives approximately $1.2 million in cash from the note but must pay out approximately $1 million in cash to the CD customer. Because all of the bank's net income was distributed as dividends, the equity available to shareholders equals the original equity of $200,000.

Table 1 – Expected Cash Flows and Income
Stable Interest Rates
(In thousands of dollars)

	Initial Cash Outlay & Book Values	Cash Flows			
		Year 1	Year 2	Year 3	Year 4
Note	-$1,200	$96	$96	$96	$1,296
CD	$1,000	-$60	-$60	-$60	-$1,060
Net Income		$36	$36	$36	$36
Dividends		-$36	-$36	-$36	-$36
Equity	$200				-$200

Table 2 shows the present value of the asset, liability, dividend, and equity cash flows, assuming that interest rates do not change. The note's cash flows are discounted at 8 percent and the CD cash flows are discounted at 6 percent. The present values for dividends (net income) and equity reflect the differences in the present value of the note and CD cash flows. These residual cash flows imply an internal rate of return on the bank's equity of 18 percent. Note that if interest rates stay at their current level, the present value of the expected cash flows equals the par value of the instruments.

Table 2 – Present Value of Expected Cash Flows and Income
Stable Interest Rates
(In thousands of dollars)

	Net Present Values	Present Value of Cash Flows			
		Year 1	Year 2	Year 3	Year 4
Note	$1,200	$88.9	$82.3	$76.2	$952.6
CD	-$1,000	-$56.6	-$53.4	-$50.4	-$839.6
Dividends & Equity	-$200	-$32.3	-$28.9	-$25.8	-$113.0

Because this bank is funding a four-year asset with an one-year liability, it is exposed to rising interest rates. Table 3 illustrates what happens to the bank's cash flows and net income if interest rates were to immediately rise by 200 basis points. The bank's reported earnings in year one remain unchanged because the bank has locked in its funding rates for the first year. After year one, however, the CD reprices by 200 basis points to a new rate of 8 percent. As a result, the bank's net income for the remaining three years will decline by $20,000 per year. The bank's cumulative net income and the corresponding dividends paid to shareholders over the four-year period declines from $144,000 to $84,000.

Table 3 – Expected Cash Flows and Income
200-Basis-Point Rise
(In thousands of dollars)

	Cash Flows			
	Year 1	Year 2	Year 3	Year 4
Note	$96	$96	$96	$1,296
CD	-$60	-$80	-$80	-$1,080
Net Income	$36	$16	$16	$16
Dividends/Equity	-$36	-$16	-$16	-$216
Change in Net Income vs. Stable Rate Scenario	$0	-$20	-$20	-$20

Table 4 illustrates the present value of the bank's expected cash flows under the new rate scenario. Note that the present value of both the note and the CD decline. The decline in the present value of the note reflects the fact that, although the cash flows from the note remain constant, those cash flows are now discounted at a higher (10 percent) rate. In essence, the bank has forgone more profitable investment opportunities and now holds a note that offers below-market returns.

As in the previous table, the present value of net income, dividends, and equity represents the difference between the present values of the note and CD cash flows. The table shows that the net economic value of the bank declines by $57.6 million in comparison with net economic value in the stable rate scenario. This decline in net economic value represents the decline in the present value of the bank's future cash flows.

Table 4 – Present Value of Expected Cash Flows and Income
200-Basis-Point Rise
(In thousands of dollars)

	Net Present Values	Present Value of Cash Flows			
		Year 1	Year 2	Year 3	Year 4
Note	$1,123.9	$87.3	$79.3	$72.1	$885.2
CD	-$981.5	-$55.6	-$68.6	-$63.5	-$793.8
Dividends & Equity	-$142.4	-$31.7	-$10.7	-$8.6	-$91.4
Change in Equity vs. Stable Rate Scenario	-$57.6				

These examples illustrate that if a bank evaluates its earnings exposure over only a short time horizon, it may incorrectly assume that it has little or no exposure. This bank shows no earnings exposure for the first 12 months. Yet, as the example illustrates, the bank's earnings in future periods may decline significantly if interest rates increase. The change in the economic value of equity (as measured by the change in the present value of the bank's assets less the present value of its liabilities) can be a leading indicator of the expected decline in future earnings and capital.

Interest Rate Risk   Appendix C

Large Bank Risk Assessment System
for Interest Rate Risk

Quantity of Interest Rate Risk

Evaluation Factors

Examiners should consider the following evaluation factors in making risk assessments. These evaluation factors, which are not a mandatory checklist, offer an overview of issues that can assist the examiner in making decisions within the risk assessment system (RAS).

When assessing the quantity of interest rate risk in an institution, examiners should consider:

- The size and stability of net interest margins and sensitive fee income.

- The component and aggregate levels of interest rate risk including repricing, basis, yield curve, and option risk relative to earnings and capital.

- Interest rate risk over both the tactical and strategic horizons.

- The vulnerability of earnings and capital under meaningful rate changes such as gradual rate shifts and yield curve twists. The appropriateness of the scenarios should be evaluated in the context of the current rate environment. Rate scenarios of sufficiently wide variability will be necessary to provide meaningful analysis (i.e., evaluation of repricing risk with a fed funds rate change of at least 200 basis points over a 12-month time horizon).

- The character of risk such as the volume and price sensitivity of various products.

- The complexity of risk positions such as the optionality of mortgage products, changing value of servicing portfolios, etc.

- The relative volume of and prospects for continued support from low-cost and stable funding sources, especially nonmaturity deposits.

Summary Assessment

Review of these factors should allow examiners to assess the quantity of interest rate risk as:

- **High** – Exposure reflects significant repricing risk; high levels of basis risk; undue yield curve risk; or significant levels of option risk. Mismatched positions are long-term and costly to hedge. The probability of substantial volatility in earnings or capital due to the movement of interest rates is high.

- **Moderate** – Exposure reflects repricing risk, basis risk, yield curve risk, and option risk that, collectively, are maintained at manageable levels. Mismatched positions may be long-term, but are effectively hedged. Substantial volatility in earnings or capital due to the movement of interest rates is not anticipated.

- **Low** – Exposure reflects little repricing risk and minimal exposure to basis risk and yield curve risk. Options positions are clearly identified and well-managed. Mismatched positions are short-term and unlikely to cause earnings or capital volatility due to the movement of interest rates.

Quality of Interest Rate Risk Management

Evaluation Factors

Examiners should consider the following evaluation factors in making risk assessments. These evaluation factors are not mandatory checklists, but rather an overview of issues that can assist the examiner in making decisions within the RAS.

Elements of interest rate risk management can be grouped into four broad categories: policies, processes, personnel, and control systems. When assessing the quality of interest rate risk management examiners should consider:

Whether policies are:

- Comprehensive, including whether they:

  –Establish responsibilities and accountabilities.
  –Specify desired limits and positions.

- Consistent with the strategic direction and risk tolerance levels.

- Approved by the board or an appropriately delegated committee, as necessary.

Whether a process exists for:

- Communicating policies and expectations to appropriate personnel.

- Approving and monitoring compliance with policy limits.

- Providing timely production and use of management information.

- Independently measuring and analyzing risk in all significant activities from interest rate movements using a variety of scenarios.

- Ensuring that risk positions are appropriately adjusted for changing market conditions and that management has sufficient expertise and market access to flexibly adjust risk levels.

- Controlling the accuracy, completeness, and integrity of data.

- Testing the reasonableness and validity of assumptions.

- Independently validating models and other measurement tools.

Whether personnel:

- Understand the source of risk, strategic direction, risk tolerance limits, and policies.

- Exhibit technical and/or managerial competency appropriate to the complexity of products.

- Are sufficient in number and skills for current and anticipated levels of risk.

- Are adequately compensated so that turnover is limited and stability is fostered.

- Demonstrate a commitment to training, development, and continuing education programs.

- Demonstrate a commitment to providing an effective performance management program.

- Ensure independence, expertise, and competency of staff performing control functions such as loan review or audit.

Whether control systems are designed to provide:

- Timely, accurate, and informative management information.

- Independent and effective feedback on compliance with policies and operating procedures. Control systems should be consistent with the complexity of the activities, but, at a minimum, should include internal and/or external audit reviews.

Summary Assessment

A review of these factors should allow examiners to assess the quality of interest rate risk management as:

- Weak – Responsible officials do not understand, or have chosen to ignore, key aspects of interest rate risk. Management does not anticipate or take timely and appropriate actions in response to changes in market conditions. Knowledge of interest rate risk may be concentrated in too few individuals in the organization. The interest rate risk management process is deficient. The process is overly simplistic in light of the relative size and complexity of the bank's on- and off-balance sheet exposures. Management information at various levels in the organization exhibits significant weaknesses. Limit structures are not reasonable, or do not reflect an understanding of the risks to earnings and the economic value of equity. Staff responsible for monitoring risk limits and measuring exposures is not independent from staff executing risk-taking decisions.

- Acceptable – Responsible officials reasonably understand the key aspects of interest rate risk. Management adequately responds to changes in market conditions. Knowledge of interest rate risk exists at appropriate levels throughout the organization. The interest rate risk management process is adequate. Measurement tools and methods may have minor weaknesses, but are appropriate given the size and complexity of the bank's on- and off-balance sheet exposures. Management information at various levels in the organization is, for the most part, timely, accurate, complete, and reliable. Limit structures are adequate to control the risk to earnings and the economic value of equity under defined and reasonable interest rate scenarios. Staff responsible for monitoring risk limits and measuring exposures are independent from staff executing risk-taking decisions.

- Strong – Responsible officials fully understand all aspects of interest rate risk. Management anticipates and responds well to changes in market conditions. Interest rate risk is well understood at all appropriate levels of the organization. The interest rate risk management process is effective and proactive. Measurement tools and methods enhance decision making by providing meaningful and timely information under a variety of defined and reasonable rate scenarios. Few, if any, weaknesses or deficiencies exist. Management information at various levels of the organization is timely, accurate, complete, and reliable. Limit structures provide clear parameters for risk to earnings and the economic value of equity under a variety of defined and reasonable interest rate scenarios. Staff responsible for monitoring risk limits and measuring exposures are independent from staff executing risk-taking decisions.

Interest Rate Risk   Appendix D

Community Bank Risk Assessment System
for Interest Rate Risk

Evaluation Factors

Examiners should consider the following evaluation factors in making risk assessments. These evaluation factors, which are not a mandatory checklist, offer an overview of issues that can assist the examiner in making decisions within the RAS.

- The size and stability of net interest margins and sensitive fee income.

- The component and aggregate levels of interest rate risk including repricing, basis, yield curve, and option risk relative to earnings and capital.

- Interest rate risk over both the short- and long-term.

- The vulnerability of earnings and capital under meaningful rate changes such as gradual rate shifts and yield curve twists. The appropriateness of the scenarios should be evaluated in the context of the current rate environment. Rate scenarios of sufficiently wide variability will be necessary to provide meaningful analysis (i.e., evaluation of repricing risk with a fed funds rate change of at least 200 basis points over a 12-month time horizon).

- The character of risk such as the volume and price sensitivity of various products.

- The complexity of risk positions such as the optionality of mortgage products, changing value of servicing portfolios, etc.

- The relative volume of and prospects for continued support from low-cost and stable funding sources, especially nonmaturity deposits.

- Whether policies or limits are approved by the board or an appropriately delegated committee, as necessary.

- How policies or limits are communicated to responsible staff.

- The existence of timely, accurate, and informative management information to monitor positions and sensitivity.

- Whether a process exists for independently measuring and analyzing risk in all significant activities from interest rate movements using a variety of scenarios.

- Whether risk positions are appropriately adjusted for changing market conditions.

- Whether management has sufficient expertise and market access to flexibly adjust risk levels.

- Testing the reasonableness and validity of assumptions and models, as necessary.

- The level and skill of management and staff.

- The existence of proper control mechanisms to monitor the accuracy of information, proper accounting treatment, and compliance with policies or laws.

Summary Assessment

Review of those factors should allow examiners to assess aggregate interest rate risk as (see next page):

As of January 12, 2012, this guidance applies to federal savings associations in addition to national banks.*

Interest Rate Risk *Low*	Interest Rate Risk *Moderate*	Interest Rate Risk *High*
Responsible officials fully understand all aspects of interest rate risk.	Responsible officials reasonably understand the key aspects of interest rate risk.	Responsible officials do not understand, or choose to ignore, key aspects of interest rate risk.
Management anticipates and responds well to changes in market conditions.	Management adequately responds to changes in market conditions.	Management does not anticipate or take timely and appropriate actions in response to changes in market conditions.
		Knowledge of interest rate risk may be concentrated in too few individuals.
Knowledge of interest rate risk is well understood at appropriate levels in the institution.	Knowledge of interest rate risk exists at appropriate levels in the institution.	
Responsibility for monitoring risk limits and measuring exposures is independent from those executing risk-taking decisions.	Responsibility for monitoring risk limits and measuring exposure is independent from those executing risk-taking decisions.	Responsibility for monitoring risk limits and measuring exposures is not independent from those executing risk-taking decisions.
Exposure reflects little repricing risk and minimal exposure to basis risk and yield curve risk. Options positions are clearly identified and well-managed.	Exposure reflects repricing risk, basis risk, yield curve risk, and option risk that, collectively, are maintained at manageable levels.	Exposure reflects significant repricing risk, high levels of basis risk, undue yield curve risk, or significant levels of option risk.
Mismatched positions are short-term.	Mismatched positions may be long-term, but are effectively hedged.	Mismatched positions are long-term and costly to hedge.
The mismatches are unlikely to cause earnings or capital volatility due to the movement of interest rates.	Substantial volatility in earnings or capital due to the movement of interest rates is not anticipated.	The probability of substantial volatility in earnings or capital due to the movement of interest rates is high.
The interest rate risk management process is effective and proactive.	Interest rate risk management process is adequate.	Interest rate risk management process is deficient.
Measurement tools and methods enhance decision making by providing meaningful and timely information under a variety of defined and reasonable rate scenarios.	Measurement tools and methods have minor weaknesses, but are appropriate given the size and complexity of the bank's on- and off-balance sheet exposures.	The process is overly simplistic in light of the relative size and complexity of the bank's on- and off-balance sheet exposures.
Management information systems are timely, accurate, complete, and reliable.	Management information is, for the most part, timely, accurate, complete and reliable.	Management information systems contain significant weaknesses.
Limit structures provide clear parameters for risk to earnings and the economic value of equity under a variety of defined and reasonable interest rate scenarios.	Limit structures are adequate to control the risk to earnings and the economic value of equity under defined and reasonable interest rate scenarios.	Limit structures are not reasonable or do not reflect an understanding of the risks to earnings and the economic value of equity.

Interest Rate Risk   Appendix E

Common Interest Rate Risk

Gap Reports

Gap reports are commonly used to assess and manage interest rate risk exposure C specifically, a bank's repricing and maturity imbalances. However, as explained later in this appendix, a basic gap report can be an unreliable indicator of a bank's overall interest rate risk exposure. Although a simple gap report does not identify and quantify basis risk, yield curve risk, and option risk, bankers have modified gap reports to do so.

Gap reports stratify all of a bank's assets, liabilities, and off-balance-sheet instruments into maturity segments (time bands) based on the instrument's next repricing or maturity date. Balances within a time band are then summed (assets are reported as positive amounts and liabilities as negative amounts) to produce a net gap position for each time band. Risk is measured by the size of the gap (the amount of net imbalance within a time band) and the length of time the gap is open.

Using properly prepared gap reports, a bank can identify and measure short- and long-term repricing imbalances. With this information, a bank can estimate its earnings and economic risks within certain constraints. Gap reports can be particularly useful in identifying the repricing risk of a bank's current balance sheet structure before assumptions are made about new business or how to effectively reinvest maturing balances.

Within a given time band, a bank may have a positive, negative, or neutral gap. A bank will have a positive gap when more assets reprice or mature than liabilities. Because this bank has more assets than liabilities subject to repricing, the bank is said to be "asset sensitive" for that time band. An asset- sensitive bank is generally expected to benefit from rising interest rates because its assets are expected to reprice more quickly than its liabilities.

As of January 12, 2012, this guidance applies to federal savings associations in addition to national banks.*

Table 1
Sample Gap Report Schedule

	< 1 Mo.	1 - 3 Mos.	3 - 6 Mos.	6 - 12 Mos.	1 - 2 Yrs.	2 - 3 Yrs.	> 3 Yrs.	Total
Loans	100	10	20	45	5	20	30	230
Investments		5	5	10	20	20	50	110
Other Assets	5						15	20
Total Assets	105	15	25	55	25	40	95	360
Nonmaturity Deposits	-65				-30		-50	-145
CDs and Other Liabilities	-35	-35	-45	-30	-10	-10	-20	-185
Total Liabilities	-100	-35	-45	-30	-40	-10	-70	-330
Equity								-30
Net Periodic Gap	5	-20	-20	25	-15	30	25	0
Cumulative Gap	5	-15	-35	-10	-25	5	30	0

A bank has a negative gap and is "liability sensitive" when more liabilities reprice within a given time band than assets. A bank that is liability-sensitive, such as the bank described in the gap report in table 1, usually benefits from falling interest rates. (The gap report in table 1 is a simplified example. In practice, most gap reports will contain many more line items and additional time bands.)

A bank whose assets equal liabilities within a time band is said to have a "neutral" gap position. A bank in a "neutral" gap position is not free of exposure to changes in interest rates, however. Although the bank's repricing risk may be small, it can still be exposed to basis risk or changes in rate relationships.

Traditionally, most bankers have used gap report information to evaluate how a bank's repricing imbalances will affect the sensitivity of its net interest income for a given change in interest rates. The same repricing information, however, can be used to assess the sensitivity of a bank's net economic value to a change in interest rates.

Construction of a Gap Report

As a general rule, all assets, liabilities, and off-balance-sheet items should be included in a bank's gap report. Less complex banks should, at a minimum, include all earning assets and interest-paying liabilities in their gap reports.

A bank also should consider including potential repricings or maturities of all nonearning assets and non-interest-bearing liabilities in its reports. Nonearning assets such as nonaccrual loans, for example, may at some point be collected or renegotiated, and then become repriceable. Non-interest-bearing liabilities (demand deposit account balances) also should be included in a bank's gap report even though such deposits do not bear an explicit rate of interest. Such deposits are included because their maturity or run-off exposes the bank to interest rate risk. (The bank may need to replace the deposits with interest-bearing sources of funds such as NOW accounts, certificates of deposits, or federal funds purchased.)

If the bank operates significant books in currencies other than the dollar, it should prepare a separate gap report for each book. Why? Interest rates in different countries can move in different directions, and the volatility of such interest rates can differ considerably as well. A significant currency book would be one that represents at least 10 percent of total business. Many banks avoid open positions or repricing imbalances in their foreign currency books. If this is the bank's policy, gap reports for those currencies may not be needed.

Number of Time Bands

A bank must decide how many time bands it will use in its gap report. In general, the narrower the time bands, the more accurate the risk measure. To measure risk to earnings, the report should have at least monthly detail over the first year and quarterly over the second. If a gap report is used to capture long-term exposures and risk to economic value, the time bands should extend to the maturity of the last asset or liability.

Time bands for distant time periods, say, beyond 10 years, may be relatively wide C five years, for example. These wider time frames are justified because the change in interest rate sensitivity is small for maturities beyond 10 years. In other words, a bank's use of wide time bands beyond 10 years will not usually cause it to misestimate its interest rate risk exposure for items in those time bands.

Reporting of Off-Balance-Sheet Items

A gap report that does not include off-balance-sheet interest rate positions does not fully measure a bank's interest rate risk profile. All material positions in off-balance-sheet instruments whose value can be affected by interest rates should be captured in a gap report. Such instruments include interest rate contracts, such as swaps, futures, and forwards; option contracts, such as caps, floors, and options on futures; and firm forward commitments to buy or sell loans, securities, or other financial instruments.

Off-balance-sheet instruments are often reported in a gap report using two entries to reflect how the instruments alter the timing of cash flows. The two entries of the contract are offsetting: one entry is the notional principal amount of the contract reported as a positive dollar value, and the other is an offsetting negative entry. If the off-balance-sheet position generally increases in value when interest rates fall (e.g., long futures, pay-floating swap, long call option, and short put option positions), the first entry is reported with a negative value and the second entry is reported with a positive value. Conversely, if the position generally increases in value when interest rates rise (e.g., short futures, pay-fixed swap, short call option, and long put option positions), the first entry is positive and the second is negative. This slotting reflects the impact of an off-balance-sheet instrument on the effective maturity of an asset on the balance sheet.

For example, if a bank has a $100 million five-year interest swap in which it receives a fixed rate and pays three-month Libor, the bank would report a positive $100 million in the five-year time band and a negative $100 million in the three-month time band. This treatment reflects the fact that the bank is Along" a fixed rate payment (as if it owned a fixed rate asset) and "short" a floating-rate payment (as if it had a floating-rate liability).

A long futures position would increase a bank's asset maturity, while a short futures position would decrease its asset maturity. Hence, a long position in a 10-year Treasury note future that expires in five months would be reported as a negative entry in the time band that covers five-month maturities and a positive entry in the time band that covers a 10-year instrument.

As discussed in the next section, option instruments such as caps and floors pose special problems for gap reports. Because most gap reports usually assume a static interest rate environment at the current level of interest rates, they ignore caps and floors until the strike rate is hit. Suppose a bank has a long position in a 10-year interest rate cap. Before the strike rate is hit, the report would show the position as a floating rate liability and would ignore the cap; after the strike rate is hit, the position becomes a 10-year fixed rate liability.

Reporting of Options-Related Positions

Many consumer products have embedded options in them because the customer has the right to change the terms of a contract or to act when warranted by market conditions. When a customer "exercises" the option, the bank loses a valuable asset that will no longer pay interest. Since these products are germane to a bank's interest rate risk exposure, institutions should incorporate them into their gap reports.

In a product with an embedded option, the cash flows will depend on the path of interest rates; different interest rate paths need to be considered because the dates of the option's exercise will change accordingly, affecting cash flows. A single gap report gives an incomplete picture of products with embedded options because it allows for only one repricing date.

Three methods of incorporating options exposures into gap reports are popular with banks. An examiner encountering a bank using another method should analyze the approach to determine whether it properly incorporates the asymmetrical impact of options on future net interest income and economic value.

The first method either recognizes that the cap is in full effect for the remaining life of the product or ignores it for that same period. The following example illustrates this all-or-nothing approach to a cap on a floating rate loan: The bank has a 10-year $100,000 floating rate loan that reprices every six months but is subject to a 12 percent lifetime cap (the rate on the loan cannot exceed 12 percent). The all-or-nothing approach would consider the loan a six-month floating rate loan when rates are below 12 percent. If rates equal or exceed 12 percent, the loan becomes a fixed rate loan with a 10-year repricing maturity.

This approach has several weaknesses. First, the method does not correctly reflect the exposure of net interest income to future changes in interest rates. For example, when the loan is slotted as a six-month repricing asset and funded with a six-month CD, the gap report would not indicate any interest rate risk. If interest rates were to rise above 12 percent, however, the loan could not reprice further but the funding costs on the CD could continue to rise, and interest rate margins would decline. Second, this treatment does not suggest how this exposure may be hedged. Neither hedging the asset as a six-month floating rate asset nor hedging it as a 10-year fixed rate asset would be appropriate.

A better approach would be for the bank to prepare two gap reports, one for a high-rate scenario and the other for a low-rate scenario. Under the high-rate scenario, the cap would be "binding" and the gap report would show the capped loans as fixed rate assets. Under the low-rate scenario, the gap report would show the loan as a floating rate asset.

A bank could use similar approaches to measure prepayment option risks associated with fixed rate residential mortgage loans. Under the high-rate scenario, the weighted average lives of the fixed rate mortgages would be extended in the gap report, reflecting the effect of slower prepayments. Under the low-rate scenario, the weighted lives would be shortened, reflecting faster prepayments. Comparing the gaps between the two schedules provides an indication of the amount of option risk the bank faces.

Although this second method provides a way to assess how embedded options may alter a bank's repricing imbalances under alternative interest rate scenarios, it also has limitations. Like the all-or-nothing approach, this method suggests that an option has value only when it becomes binding or is in the money. In reality, an option has value throughout its life. The value of the option will depend on such factors as the time to expiration of the option, the distance from the strike price, and the volatility of interest rates.

A third approach for incorporating options into gap reports varies the value of the option according to the change in the value of the underlying instrument. This is done by incorporating the delta-equivalent value of the option into the gap report. The delta-equivalent value of an option, a mathematically derived weighting between 0 percent and 100 percent, reflects the probability that the option will go in the money.

In the illustration of the loan with the 12 percent lifetime cap described above, the bank could "strip" the cap from the loan and treat the cap and loan as two separate instruments. The bank would report the loan as a six-month floating rate loan and the cap as an off-balance-sheet instrument, based on the cap's delta-equivalent value. The delta-equivalent value would equal the delta of the cap times the notional value of the cap (in this case, the principal amount of the loan, or $100,000).

The cap in this example would have a delta between 50 percent and 100 percent when rates are greater than 12 percent. The high level of the delta indicates a high probability of the cap being effective over the life of the loan. If market rates were at 8 percent, however, the delta would be much lower, reflecting a lower probability that the cap will be effective over the life of the loan.

The delta approach also has limitations. The delta of an option changes in a nonlinear fashion with the passage of time and with the level of interest rates. As a result, the delta value of an option is valid only for small changes in interest rates, and this value changes over time.

Measuring Risk to Net Interest Income

After a bank has stratified the bank's assets, liabilities, and off-balance-sheet instruments into time bands and determined how it will treat embedded options, it must measure net interest income (NII) at risk. The formula to translate gaps into the amount of net interest income at risk, measuring exposure over several periods, is:

(Periodic gap) x (change in rate) x (time over which the periodic gap is in effect) = change in NII

This formula can be illustrated by applying it to the sample gap report shown in table 1 and calculating the change in the bank's net interest income for an immediate 200-basis-point increase in rates. For example, the bank has a negative gap of $20 million in the one-month to three-month time band. This means that more liabilities than assets will reprice or mature during this time frame. Hence, for the remaining 10 months of the bank's 12-month time horizon, the bank will have $20 million more of liabilities than assets that have repriced at higher (200 basis points higher) rates. As shown in table 2, the increase in rates reduces the bank's earnings for the 10-month period by approximately $333,000. The cumulative earnings effect of the bank's repricing imbalances over the 12-month horizon is a reduction in net interest income of approximately $362,500.

Table 2
Sample Net Interest Income Sensitivity Calculation

Time Band	Size of Gap (In Millions of Dollars)	Basis Point Change	Part of Year Gap Is in Effect*	Impact on Annualized NII (In Thousands of Dollars)
< 1 Month	$ 5	200	11.5/12	$95.8
1 - 3 Months	-$20	200	10/12	-$333.3
3 - 6 Months	-$20	200	7.5/12	-$250.0
6 - 12 Months	$25	200	3/12	$125.0
Total				-$362.5

* Assumes all repricings occur at midpoint of time band

It is important to stress that this method of measuring a bank's net interest income at risk is very crude and employs numerous simplifying assumptions, including the following:

- All repricing and maturities within a time band occur simultaneously (as in the above formula), typically at the beginning, middle, or end of the period.
- All maturing assets and liabilities are reinvested at overnight rates.
- No other new business is booked.
- There is an instantaneous change in the overnight rate to a new and constant level.
- All interest rates move the same amount. The sensitivity of the results to these assumptions can be tested by using simulation models.

Measuring Risk to Economic Value

Gap reports may be used to measure the exposure of a bank's net economic value to a change in interest rates. To do so, a bank multiplies the balances in each time band by a price sensitivity factor that approximates, for a given change in interest rates, the percentage change in the present value of an instrument with similar cash flow and maturity characteristics. For example, consider a bank that has $10 million of two-year Treasury notes slotted in the time band covering from two years to three years in its gap report. To estimate the market value sensitivity of those balances to a 200-basis-point increase in market interest rates, a banker would multiply those balances by a factor that approximates the change in the present value of a two-year Treasury note for a 200-basis-point movement in rates. The present value of a note with a 7.5 percent coupon would decline 3.6 percent for such a rate movement. Hence, the estimated decline in the market value of the bank's $10 million two-year Treasury note would be approximately $360,000 ($10 million times negative 3.6 percent).

Similar price sensitivity factors can be applied to other types of instruments and time bands. The exposure of the bank's net economic value would be the sum of the weighted balances.

Limitations of Gap Reports

Basis Risk

The focus of a gap report is on the level of net repricings. The assumption is that within a given time band, assets and liabilities fully offset or "hedge" each other. In practice, however, assets and liabilities price off different yield curves or indices and do not move at all points together.

To facilitate an interpretation of basis risk, some bankers group instruments with similar basis relationships into separate line items within the report and report average rates and yields on those groups. For example, within a 30- to 60-day time band, the repricing imbalance for accounts tied to CD rates could be reported as one line item, followed by balances tied to the Treasury curve. This approach provides a rough approximation of the degree of basis risk present in the balance sheet.

Alternatively, some banks prepare *beta-adjusted* gap reports in an attempt to measure basis risk. In this type of report, the repricing balance for each account type is multiplied by a factor that approximates the correlation between that account's pricing behavior and a benchmark market interest rate. For example, the report could compare the pricing behavior for all accounts to the federal funds rate. If the analysis revealed that the bank's pricing on money market deposit accounts moves 50 basis points for every 100-basis-point movement in the federal funds rate, 50 percent of such balances would be shown as short-term rate-sensitive, and the remaining balances would be assigned a longer maturity.

Even beta-adjusted gap reports, however, do not always provide a complete picture of a bank's basis risk because the correlation between account pricing and market interest rates may not be the same for rising and declining interest rate environments or even for similar rate environments at different points in time. In such cases, a bank may need to formulate different correlations or "beta" factors for each rate scenario it develops.

Given the limitations of gap reports, intuition and judgment are required when using them to quantify the exposure of earnings to changes in interest rates.

Yield Curve Risk

To measure a bank's cumulative repricing risk over several periods or time bands, most users of gap reports simply sum the gaps across each time band to produce a net cumulative gap position. Implicit in this act is an assumption that movements in interest rates will be perfectly correlated across the time bands and will move in a parallel fashion. This assumption can be amended by applying different weights to each time band. For example, gaps in the shorter time bands could be weighted more heavily than those in the longer time bands because short-term interest rates are usually more volatile and usually move by larger amounts than long-term rates.

The pattern of a bank's repricing gaps across the various time bands can provide an indication of the bank's exposure to changes in yield curve shapes. Suppose a bank that is liability sensitive (has negative gaps) in the short- and long-term time bands and asset sensitive in the intermediate time bands is exposed to a flattening of the yield curve when short-term rates go up and long-term rates remain stable. The bank's net interest margin deteriorates as the rates on its short-term liabilities increase. Because long-term rates remain stable, however, the market value of its long-term liabilities remain constant. Hence, the bank will not benefit from a decline in the expected future value of its long-term obligations.

Option Risks

As noted in earlier discussions, it is difficult to capture option risks with gap reports. Options introduce an asymmetrical and nonlinear element to a bank's risk profile. Although techniques such as preparing multiple gap reports and reporting options by their delta-equivalent values attempt to overcome some of these weaknesses, they are unable to fully capture all of the dimensions of option risk. To do so, a bank that has significant option risk must supplement its gap reports with simulation or option pricing models.

Intra-Period Gaps

Although gap reports rely on stratifying balances into broad time bands, they do not detect imbalances within those bands. Some bankers have partly overcome this weakness by reporting the weighted average repricing maturity within each time band. Another method is to reduce the width of the bands.

New Business

Many gap reports used by banks consider only the bank's current financial positions. These reports are called "static" reports because they capture only the risk that arises from the bank's existing balance sheet structure and do not incorporate any assumptions about new business. Some banks may also prepare "dynamic" gap reports. Typically, these reports are generated from the bank's earnings simulation models and show how the bank's "gap" would appear at some point in the future, after new business assumptions are incorporated into the risk measure.

Bank Simulation Models

Simulation models may be used for measuring interest rate risk arising from current and future business scenarios. They can be used to measure risk from either an earnings or economic perspective. The models "simulate" or project a bank's risk exposure under a variety of assumptions and scenarios and, thus, can be used to isolate sources of a bank's risk exposure or quantify certain types of risk. To do so, a bank performs a series of simulations and applies different assumptions and scenarios to each simulation.

In general, earnings simulation models are more dynamic than gap analyses and market valuation simulations. Whereas gap and market valuation models generally take a "snapshot" of the risk inherent in a bank's balance sheet structure at a particular point in time, most earnings simulation models evaluate risk exposure over a period of time, taking into account projected changes in balance sheet structures, pricing, and maturity relationships, and assumptions about new business.

Banks often use simulation models to analyze alternative business decisions and to test the effect of those decisions on a bank's risk profile before implementation. Banks also use simulation models in budgeting and profit planning processes.

Construction of a Simulation Model

Most simulation models are computer-based models that perform a series of calculations under a range of scenarios and assumptions. From data on the bank's current position and managerial assumptions about future interest rate movements, customer behavior, and new business, a simulation model projects future cash flows, income, and expenses. These assumptions include different loan growth and funding plan scenarios and other assumptions about how a bank's assets and liabilities will be replaced. The main components of a simulation model are presented in the table below.

Earnings Simulation Model
Basic Structure

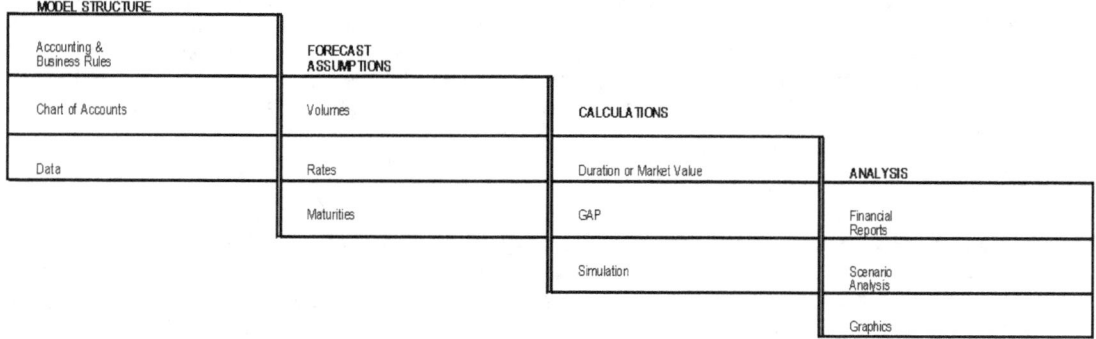

Data from a bank's general ledger and transaction systems generally provide information on the bank's current position for each portfolio in the model's chart of accounts. This information is similar to that used for a gap report and includes current balances, rates, and repricing and maturity schedules. New business and reinvestment plans, which are generally more subjective, are based on management's assumptions. Those assumptions might be derived from historical trends, business plans, or econometrics models. Both market interest rates and business mix are forecasted.

Forecasts of interest rates involve forecasts of their direction, the future shape of the yield curve, and the relationship between the various indices that the bank uses for pricing products.

The bank's potential exposure is estimated by calculating how a change in rates will affect the value, income, and expense of the bank's current and forecasted financial positions.

The output of a typical simulation model consists of: 1) future balance sheet and income statements under a number of interest rate and business-mix scenarios; 2) an analysis of the impact of the different scenarios on the value of the target account; and 3) graphical representations of the analysis that are often used to communicate results to senior management and the board.

Measurement of Risk

The greater the interest rate risk, the greater the change in the value of a targeted account under different interest rate scenarios. The target account is usually net interest income or net income. Many simulation models also are capable of measuring changes in the market value of equity. Several business-mix and rate scenarios usually are run. Rate scenarios often include rising, flat, and declining rates, as well as a most probable scenario.

Table 3 illustrates the type of summary report that may be generated by an earnings simulation model. The report shows variation in net interest income under alternative interest rate scenarios using a flat rate scenario as a base. Similar reports are often developed to show how net interest income might vary with alternative business mixes and strategies.

Table 3
Net Interest Income Sensitivity
(In millions of dollars)

	NII Flat	Change in NII	
		Up 200 BP	Down 200 BP
Qtr 1	100	-5	5
Qtr 2	90	-5	5
Qtr 3	95	-10	15
Qtr 4	110	-10	15
Total	395	-30	40

A bank might have risk limits that restrict losses in the account at risk for a defined interest rate scenario over a certain period of time. For example, the bank in the table above might limit losses in annual net interest income from a 200 basis point change in rates to 10 percent of its base net interest income.

Advantages of Simulation Models

Simulation models allow some of the assumptions underlying gap reports to be amended. For instance, gap reports assume a one-time shift in interest rates. Simulation models can handle varying interest rate paths, including variations in the shape of the yield curve. Gap reports usually assume the improbable C that all current assets and liabilities run off and are reinvested overnight. Simulation models can be more realistic. A simulation model can accommodate various business forecasts and allow flexibility in running sensitivity analyses. For instance, basis risk can be evaluated by varying the spreads between the indices the bank uses to price its products.

Perhaps the strongest advantage of simulation models is that they can present risk in terms that are meaningful and clear to senior management and boards of directors. The results of simulation models present risk and reward under alternative rate scenarios in terms of net interest income, net income, and present value (economic value of equity). These terms are basic financial fundamentals that are readily understood by bank management.

Simulation models can vary greatly in their complexity and accuracy. As the cost of computing technology has declined, simulation models have improved. Some simulation models can:

- Handle the intermediate principal amortizations of products such as installment loans.
- Handle caps and floors on adjustable rate loans and prepayments of mortgages or mortgage-backed securities under various interest rate scenarios (embedded options).
- Handle nonstandard swaps and futures contracts.
- Change spread relationships to capture basis risk.
- Model a variety of interest rate movements and yield curve shapes.
- Test for internal consistency among assumptions.
- Analyze market or economic risk as well as risk to interest income.

Limitations of Simulation Models

Although offering greater versatility than the alternatives, simulation is not always objective. A simulation can misrepresent the bank's current risk position because it relies on management's assumptions about the bank's future business.

The myriad of assumptions that underlie most simulation models can make it difficult to determine how much a variable contributes to changes in the value of the target account. For this reason, many banks supplement their earnings simulation measures by isolating the risk inherent in the existing balance sheet using gap reports or measurements of risk to the economic value of equity.

In measuring their earnings at risk, many bankers limit the evaluation of their risk exposures to the following two years because interest rate and business assumptions that project further are considered unreliable. As a result, banks that use simulation models with horizons of only one or two years do not fully capture their long-term exposure. A bank that uses a simulation model to measure the risk solely to near-term earnings should supplement its model with gap reports or economic value of equity models that measure the amount of long-term repricing exposures.

Economic Value Sensitivity and Duration Models

Techniques that measure economic value sensitivity can capture the interest rate risk of the bank's business mix across the spectrum of maturities. Economic value sensitivity systems generally compute and measure changes in the present value of the bank's assets, liabilities, and off-balance-sheet accounts under alternative interest rate scenarios.

Construction of Economic Value Models

Most economic value measurement systems are a form of simulation model. Typically, these models first estimate the current or "base case" present value of all of the bank's assets, liabilities, and off-balance-sheet accounts. The model projects the amount and timing of the cash flows that are expected to be generated by the bank's financial instruments under the Abase case" interest rate scenario. These cash flows are then discounted by an appropriate discount factor to arrive at a net present value.

For the "base case" scenario, the bank's net economic value equals the present value of expected cash flows from the bank's assets, minus the present value of expected cash flows from the bank's liabilities, plus or minus the present value of expected cash inflows from the bank's off-balance-sheet positions.

To measure the sensitivity of the bank's economic exposure to changes in interest rates, the model then performs similar calculations of expected discounted cash flows for alternative interest rate scenarios. The level and timing of cash flows for products with option features will often vary with each rate scenario being evaluated. For example, the rate of mortgage prepayments increases as interest rates decrease.

Measurement of Risk

For alternative scenarios, the change in net economic value from the base case represents the interest rate sensitivity of the bank's net economic value. The greater the change in net economic value, the greater the potential risk exposure of the bank.

Table 4 illustrates the type of output that is generated by economic value sensitivity models. In this example, the economic value of the bank's equity would be adversely affected by a rise in interest rates. For example, if rates rose by 200 basis points, the present value of the bank's assets would decline by $2.5 million, whereas the present value of the bank's liabilities would decline by only $1.5 million. As a result, the bank's net economic value would decline by $1 million from the base scenario.

Table 4
Sample Output of Economic Value Simulation Model

Interest Rate Scenario
(In thousands of dollars)

	Down 200 BP	Down 100 BP	Base Case	Up 100 BP	Up 200 BP
PV of Assets	$55,000	$54,500	$53,500	$52,000	$51,000
Change	$1,500	$1,000	$0	($1,500)	($2,500)
PV of Liabilities	$ 49,000	$48,700	$48,000	$ 47,000	$46,500
Change	$1,000	$700	$0	($1,000)	($1,500)
PV of Equity	$ 6,000	$5,800	$5,500	$5,000	$4,500
Change	$500	$300	$0	$(500)	($1,000)

Duration [1]

Many economic sensitivity models also compute the duration of a bank's financial instruments. Duration is a measure of the sensitivity of market values to small changes in interest rates. If interest rates increase, the market value of a fixed income instrument will decline. Duration indicates by how much. The duration of a fixed income instrument that has no option features is the percentage change in the market value of the instrument from a change in market rates. For instance, the market value of a bond with a duration of five will decline by roughly 0.5 percent if interest rates increase by 10 basis points.

Before advances in computing technology made simulations of net present values under multiple interest rate scenarios feasible, some bankers used duration as a proxy for estimating the net economic value of their institution. Duration is still used by many bank managers as a basis for evaluating the relative risks of different financial instruments, portfolios, or investment strategies.

---

[1] Duration was derived from calculus by Frederick Macaulay in 1938 as a means to compare the maturities of instruments with differing payment structures, such as amortizing versus nonamortizing bonds. This became known as Macaulay's duration. Later, this measure was modified to express the price sensitivity of a bond to a given percentage change in interest rates; this is known as modified duration. Modified duration is simply duration divided by (1   (market yield/ the number of coupon payments per year)). In this section, the term duration will refer to modified duration and will focus on its use as a measure of market value sensitivity.

Duration incorporates an instrument's remaining time to maturity, the level of interest rates, and intermediate cash flows. If a fixed income instrument has only one cash flow, as a zero coupon bond does, duration will equal the maturity of the instrument a zero coupon bond with five years remaining to maturity has a duration of five years. If coupon payments are received before maturity, the duration of the bond declines, reflecting the fact that some cash is received before final maturity. For example, a five-year 10 percent coupon bond has a duration of 4.2 years in a 10 percent interest rate environment.

Duration is calculated by weighting the present value of an instrument's cash flows by the time to receipt of those cash flows. Table 5 illustrates the calculation of the Macaulay and modified durations of a $100,000 two-year note that pays interest semiannually, has a 7.5 percent coupon, and was purchased at par to yield 7.5 percent. This note has a modified duration of 1.82. If rates were to increase 100 basis points, the value of this note would be expected to decline by approximately 1.82 percent.

Table 5
Sample Duration Calculation

Period (t)	Cash Flow	PV of $1 at 3.75 percent*	PV of CF	t x PV of CF
1	$3,750	0.96386	$3,614	$3,614
2	$3,750	0.92902	$3,484	$6,968
3	$3,750	0.89544	$3,358	$10,074
4	$103,750	0.86307	$89,544	$358,176
Total			$100,000	$378,832
Macaulay Duration: $378,832/$100,000 = 3.79 semiannual periods or 1.89 years				
Modified Duration: 1.89/(1+(7.50%/2) = 1.89/(1+0.0375) = 1.82				
* A 3.75% coupon and discount rate is used, because the semiannual payment of interest.				

The calculations in table 5 do not adjust the expected cash flows of the bond to changes in interest rates. Hence, this calculation (modified duration) is not valid for instruments, such as callable bonds and mortgage-backed securities, whose options will change their cash flows as interest rates move. To correct for this problem, many banks use what has become known as "effective duration." Effective duration is derived by using simulation techniques to calculate the change in price of an instrument for a given change in interest rates. The concepts of effective duration and convexity are discussed in more detail in a later section.

Properties of Duration

In general, duration exhibits the following characteristics:

- The higher the duration, the greater the price sensitivity of the instrument to changes in market interest rates.
- For two instruments with the same maturity, a high-coupon instrument will have a lower duration than a low-coupon instrument and will also be less price sensitive. A larger proportion of a high coupon's cash flows will be received sooner and thus the average time to receipt of the cash flows will be less.
- A given fixed income instrument will have a higher duration in a low interest rate environment than in a high interest rate environment.
- Duration may be positive or negative. A fixed rate instrument would have a positive duration, and an increase in interest rates would generally decrease the market value of the instrument. Mortgage servicing rights and interest-only (IO) mortgage-backed securities generally have a negative duration, since an increase in interest rates would

decrease the prepayment speed of the underlying mortgages, increasing the market value of the instruments.
- Durations are additive when weighted by the amount of the contract. For example, if a portfolio consists of two bonds of equal market value, one with a duration of six and the other with a duration of two, the duration of the portfolio would be four.

Duration Can Measure the Exposure of a Portfolio of Instruments

Duration can measure the exposure of the economic value of a single contract or a portfolio of contracts carried at market value. The duration of a portfolio of contracts can be calculated by computing the weighted average maturity of all the cash flows in the portfolio individually. However, because the duration of individual instruments is usually readily available, most banks estimate the duration of a portfolio of contracts by weighting the durations of the individual contracts and summing them.

Many banks use duration to measure and limit the risk of a portfolio of fixed income contracts. This measurement is much more precise than simply limiting the amount of securities with certain maturities a bank may hold. Duration also allows portfolio managers to combine the risks of different contracts based on their price sensitivity and to hedge the net risk of the portfolio.

Table 6 illustrates how duration may be used to calculate the interest rate risk of a portfolio of fixed income contracts.

Table 6
Duration of a Portfolio of Instruments

Instrument	Yield to Maturity	Price/Amount	Modified Duration	Weighted Duration
7.5% coupon, 2-year note	10%	$95,567	1.80	.60
8% coupon, 5-year note	10%	$92,278	3.98	1.28
10% coupon, 10-year note	10%	$100,000	6.23	2.16
Duration of Portfolio:				4.04

The weighted duration of the portfolio is 4.04. If interest rates were to increase by 1 percent, the market value of the portfolio would decline by about approximately 4.04 percent or $11,629.

Duration Can Measure the Economic Value of Equity

Some banks use duration to measure or hedge the sensitivity of the economic value of their portfolio equity to changes in interest rates. The duration of equity is derived from the duration of all assets, liabilities, and off-balance-sheet contracts.

To understand how the duration of equity measures risk, the economic value of portfolio equity may be viewed as a net bond position. Assets are analogous to long bond positions with positive durations, and liabilities are analogous to short bond positions with negative durations. Duration indicates whether the economic value of the net bond position C or portfolio equity C will increase or decrease with a change in rates.

A bank with long-term assets funded by short-term liabilities will generally have a duration of equity that is positive. The economic value of portfolio equity of this bank will decline as interest rates rise. A bank with short-term assets funded with long-term liabilities will generally have a negative duration of equity. The economic value of this bank will increase as interest rates rise. The higher the duration of a bank's equity (whether the number is positive or negative), the more sensitive is its economic value to changes in rates.

Advantages of Duration

Duration is a useful tool for setting risk limits either on the net economic value of the bank or for selected portfolios, such as investment portfolios. Some banks attempt to limit their economic exposures through simple position limits, which are usually based on maturity. Such limits, however, do not precisely assess the sensitivity of market values to changes in rates, something limits based on duration can do.

Limits based on duration analysis are best expressed in terms of dollar changes in market or economic value. Duration measures the percentage change in value rather than the actual dollar change. To calculate exposure of the account at risk (the economic value of equity), a bank must weight the durations of assets, liabilities, and off-balance-sheet accounts by their economic values.

Limitations of Duration

Duration as a measure of the sensitivity of economic value also has limitations:

- Macaulay and modified duration accurately measure changes in value for small and generally parallel changes in interest rates. However, modified duration can not measure changes in value for nonparallel changes in interest rates, and there is no practical method by which effective duration can measure nonparallel shifts. The margin of error, which increases with the size of the interest rate change, is called convexity.
- The duration of different instruments will change at different rates as time passes (duration drift). In other words, in a portfolio hedged for duration the effectiveness of the hedge will diminish over time.
- Macaulay and modified duration assume that the expected cash flows of a fixed income instrument will not change with interest rate movement. Hence, these duration measures are not accurate for instruments with embedded options, which often grow more sensitive to interest rates as rates rise. In other words, an instrument that declines in value by 1 percent for a 100-basis-point increase in interest rates might decline by 3 percent for a 200-basis-point increase and by 6 percent for a 300-basis-point increase.

Convexity and Effective Duration

Banks can adjust modified duration to overcome some of the problems of convexity. Effective duration incorporates changes in cash flow that occur in instruments with options. (Convexity reflects a nonlinear shift in the price/yield relationships of instruments with and without options.) However, effective duration is useful only for a specific interest rate change. To obtain an instrument's effective duration, calculate its present values at two different market yields and obtain the percentage change in price (PV and PV.). Divide the absolute difference between the two present values by the bond's original (base-case) market price (PV) times the assumed change in yield (y) times two:

$$\frac{(PV_- - PV_+)}{2PVy}$$

The resulting number is the instrument's effective duration.

For example, a bank can calculate the effective duration of a Government National Mortgage Association security after a 100-basis-point rise in interest rates. Assume the security is currently trading at par to yield 7 percent. The bank first estimates the present value of the security if interest rates increase to 8 percent. In calculating this present value the bank takes into account that the cash flows of this security will increase because prepayments will slow. The present value at 8 percent (PV_+) is $94. Then the bank estimates the present value at 6 percent (PV_-), taking into account the decrease in cash flows because the rate of prepayment is higher. The present value at 6 percent (PV_-) is $104. The bond's effective duration [($104 - $94 / 2 (100) (.01)] is 5. In other words, the bond's value will decline by approximately 5 percent for the 100-basis-point increase in interest rates.

(The formula used to estimate an option-free fixed income instrument's convexity is provided in a technical note at the end of this appendix.)

Monte Carlo Simulation

Monte Carlo simulation measures the probable outcomes of events, such as a movement in interest rates, that have a random or stochastic element.

The simulation models discussed previously measure the value of the bank under a limited number of interest rate scenarios. Such approaches are "deterministic" because the possible interest rate paths are predetermined and controlled by the model user. Although deterministic models are valuable, their outcomes depend on the interest rate scenarios. If actual interest rates differ from assumptions, the risk to the bank may be substantially different from the measured risk.

The outcome of a Monte Carlo simulation is less preordained than that of a deterministic simulation because its statistical modeling technique generates thousands of randomly determined interest rate paths. These interest rate paths result in a distribution of possible interest rate scenarios. The value of the bank or the bank's portfolios is then evaluated for each of the possible interest rate paths, yielding a range of possible values or outcomes.

Construction of a Monte Carlo Simulation

Formulating the average Monte Carlo model is quite complex:

(1) The first step is to develop the underlying probability distribution for interest rates that will generate the random interest rate paths. Typically, the current forward yield curve is used to anchor the probability distribution.

(2) A model generates a multitude of random interest rate paths (typically several thousand). However, certain properties are usually built into this process to ensure that the mean (average) interest rate generated is consistent with the current structure of interest rates and that the dispersion (distribution) of possible interest rates is consistent with observed volatility. These properties are important to ensure that the model does not introduce the possibility of Arisk-free" arbitrage. Essentially, the properties assume that markets efficiently and fairly price securities, such that one cannot construct instruments with equivalent risk and higher returns than what the market commands.

(3) The cash flows corresponding to each of the randomly developed interest rate paths are calculated. That is, the bank specifies the relationships between the interest rates and the cash flows of the bank's portfolios. For example, the bank would develop a prepayment function that relates mortgage prepayments with each interest rate path. Once adjusted for prepayments and other interest-rate effects, the cash flows are said to be "option-adjusted."

(4) The option-adjusted cash flows for each rate path are discounted by the risk-free rate to obtain their net present value. All of these outcomes are summed, and the total is divided by the total number of rate paths evaluated to produce an expected net present value for the distribution. If the cash flows have been adjusted correctly and the interest rate paths correctly reflect market expectations about the distribution of possible future interest rates outcomes, this expected net present value represents the base-case market price. If the model's assumptions are accurate, the cash flows have been adjusted for all risks, and the market for the instrument under consideration operates according to the underlying theory (which assumes risk neutral valuation), this base-case price should be within a few basis points of observable market prices. If the net present value does not match the market price, common practice is to add a fixed spread known as the option-adjusted spread (OAS) to the risk-free rate.

(5) After obtaining the base-case price in step 4, the current forward yield curve is "shocked" for each of the interest rate scenarios that banks consider in their risk analysis. For example, if the bank is evaluating its risk for a parallel 200-basis-point increase in rates, it would shift the underlying distribution of interest rates (developed in step 1) by 200 basis points such that the expected mean (average) is 200 basis points higher across the maturity spectrum. Steps 2,3, and 4 are then repeated, except that the "market price" that results represents the price that would result if interest rates were to change as assumed for that rate scenario. The resulting estimates are used to fill in a report such as the one illustrated in table 4.

Advantages of Monte Carlo Simulation

Monte Carlo simulation is a powerful risk analysis tool because it alone, of the tools discussed in this booklet, can accurately and clearly adjust risk estimates for optionality and convexity. The capital markets employ Monte Carlo techniques to price interest rate derivative products and residential mortgage products using OAS analysis. Banks can employ Monte Carlo techniques to understand and evaluate current market pricing as well as their economic value at risk. This technique provides banks with a valuable tool for measuring and managing interest rate risk. "Investment Securities" in the *Comptroller's Handbook* discusses how to compare securities using OAS analysis.

Limitations of Monte Carlo Simulation

Monte Carlo simulations, like all interest rate risk measurement systems, are only as good as the data and assumptions underlying the analysis. Two critical assumptions in Monte Carlo analysis are the process used to derive the interest rate paths and the cash flow relationships developed for each interest rate path. If these assumptions are faulty, the results of the simulation will be suspect. Monte Carlo simulations are complicated to develop and require substantial computing technology. To correctly derive and apply this modeling process, a bank must have staff members with considerable expertise in financial and statistical theory.

Model Exposure

Regardless of the type of model used, banks should take care to minimize model exposure. Financial models fall into error for many reasons. Users may make incorrect assumptions about deposit behavior or about changes in the spread between interest rates. They may select a model that is not appropriate for all parameters. A model that provides reasonable results for a certain range of inputs may fail to do so for extreme assumptions. Some model users misuse good models; for example, they evaluate an insufficient number of paths, in the process sacrificing accuracy for the sake of speed. When designers fail to provide adequate documentation, they increase the possibility that future changes to the model will result in errors.

Technical Note: Calculating Convexity

The convexity of an option-free fixed income instrument is measured by the following formula:

$$\text{Convexity (in periods)} = \frac{1(2)PVCF_1 + 2(3)PVCF_2 + 3(4)PVCF_3 + \ldots + n(n+1)PVCF_n}{(1+y)^2 \times PVTCF}$$

Where:

$PVCF_t$ = Present value of the cash flow in period t discounted at the prevailing period yield
t = Period when the cash flow is expected to be received
n = Number of periods until maturity
$PVTCF$ = Total present value of the bond

One can estimate how much, in percent, convexity can change the price of an option-free instrument:

Approximate change in price (in percent)=
(.5) x convexity (in years) x (yield change)^2 x 100

Table 7 calculates the convexity of the 7.5 percent coupon bond shown in table 5 and how much, in percent, this convexity will change the bond's price.

Table 7
Sample Convexity Calculation

Period (t)	t(t+1)	PVCF$_t$	t(t+1) PVCF$_t$
1	2	$3,614	$7,228
2	6	$3,484	$20.904
3	12	$3,358	$40,296
4	20	$89,544	$1,790,880
Total		$100,000	$1,859,308
$(1+y)^2 \times PVTCF = (1.0375)^2 \times \$100,000 = \$107,640.62$			
Convexity (semiannual) =($1,859,308)/($107,640.62) = 17.27			
Convexity (in years) = (convexity in periods)/(# of periods)^2 = 17.27/4 = 4.318			
Change in price (in percent) because of convexity after a 100-basis-point increase in rates: (.5)(4.318)(.01)^2 x 100 = .02%			

The total change in price, in percent, of the 7.5 coupon bond after a 100-basis-point move can now be estimated by summing the changes caused by modified duration and convexity. (For option-free bonds, convexity will always have a positive effect on price, and duration will have a negative effect.) Thus, the 7.5 coupon bond is estimated to decline by 1.80 percent (duration of minus 1.82 percent plus convexity of 0.02 percent) after a 100-basis-point increase in rates. If rates decrease by 100 basis points, the bond is estimated to increase in price by 1.84 percent (duration of 1.82 percent plus convexity of 0.02 percent).

Interest Rate Risk

Appendix F

Interest Rate Risk Models: In-House or Vendor?

A bank may either design and develop risk measurement models internally or purchase them from an outside vendor. Developing an in-house model (if the bank has the ability) is often preferable because the model can be tailored to the bank's unique business mix.

To develop its own model, a bank must be able to commit sufficient money and staff members to ensure the integrity of the model's design and algorithm and to maintain the model. Because as few as one or two employees may come to be the bank's acknowledged experts on the in-house model, management should ensure that there is sufficient documentation to enable others to maintain and support the model in the absence of these key employees.

Using a model developed by a third-party vendor can reduce resource requirements, as well as start-up times and costs. For banks with limited staff resources, some vendor models may offer a fuller and more comprehensive risk measurement system than what the bank could develop internally. The use of vendor models may free the bank's staff from programming efforts and allow more resources to be devoted to the qualitative issues of interest rate risk management.

But some banks have found even external models costly to implement. Vendor models may not be able to capture all of the types of instruments the bank holds or all facets of a bank's risk exposure. Vendor models can become "black boxes" to inexperienced users, who obtain output without fully understanding the modeling process. This imperfect knowledge can produce undetected errors and misleading or incorrect results.

Before selecting a model, a bank must determine what model features it needs and examine alternative packages based on those needs. Above all, management should consider the ability of bank personnel to understand and update the model. Selecting a model that is too complex for staff members can stymie interest rate risk management.

The OCC expects banks to have systems in place that can identify, measure, monitor, and control the major sources of the bank's interest rate risk exposure. A bank's model should be able to handle every type of financial instrument (on- and off-balance-sheet) that the bank uses. For example, the model selected by a bank holding adjustable rate mortgages should be able to handle periodic and lifetime caps on interest rates, different prepayment estimates, as well as the calculation of amortization schedules.

Management should ensure that the reports generated by the model are easy to prepare and interpret. If the bank will use the model in its budgeting and planning process, the model should be able to track and compare actual results with projections.

Banks should consider the type of hardware needed to run the model or software package. Will the model be run on a personal computer or the bank's mainframe? How long will it take to run the model? Will the model expend so much computer time that the production of other computer-generated reports will be compromised?

When considering models supplied by outside vendors, management should evaluate the financial strength of the vendor as well as the support the vendor will provide. Bank management should find out whether the vendor will supply initial and ongoing support using hotlines, training, and consultants; how frequently the software will be updated, how the bank will obtain the updates, and how the vendor validates models and new software releases; and how the vendor supports older releases of a product that has been updated.

How easy is it for model users to discover and track errors? A model that can flag inconsistent data, say, when a user inputs a level of maturity balances that exceeds outstanding current balances, facilitates the early discovery of errors. Comprehensive documentation on the model's operation should help track errors.

Bank management should also consider:

- Whether the bank needs a menu-driven system or one that is programming oriented. Although menus are generally more user-friendly, systems with programming capabilities may be more flexible.
- The number of accounts and different products that a model can accommodate to ensure that the model meets the bank's current and projected needs.
- Whether the bank as well as the vendor can add or modify accounts analyzed by the model.
- Whether the time periods (months, quarters, years) that the model can project fit the structure of the bank's balance sheet.
- How many interest rate scenarios the model can run and whether the scenarios are generic or can be specified by

the bank.

- How many "driver" market interest rates and yield curves the model allows.
- Whether the process by which data is input into the model preserves the data's accuracy and integrity. Management should consider how much data must be inputted and whether it must be manually entered or can be extracted directly from the bank's operating systems. In a multibank holding company structure, management also should consider whether the model permits the consolidation of data.
- The types of analyses that the model is capable of producing, such as gap reports and comparisons of net income under alternative interest rate scenarios.
- Whether the model can calculate duration and market valuations.
- Whether the vendor has staff members who can prepare special reports at the bank's request in addition to standard reports.

Interest Rate Risk

Appendix G

Nonmaturity Deposit Assumptions

Background

The assumptions a bank makes about nonmaturity deposits, such as demand deposit accounts (DDA), negotiable order of withdrawal (NOW) accounts, savings accounts, and money market demand accounts (MMDA), are probably the most important ones to be made in developing gap, simulation, and economic valuation models. These deposits usually represent a large proportion of a bank's funding base.

Banks make different assumptions about the repricing sensitivity and maturity structure of nonmaturity deposits. For example, some banks consider MMDAs to be fully rate-sensitive and assign them a short maturity because the bank may at any time elect to change the rates paid on those funds. Other banks liken MMDAs to fixed rate funds with longer maturities because management generally does not change the rate paid on the deposits.

Some banks view their nonmaturity deposits as products with embedded options whose maturity or repricing will depend on the behavior of customers and competitors and the pricing policies of bank management. Because of these embedded options, management's assumptions can change with the interest rate scenario.

The OCC does not dictate which assumptions or methods banks must use to assess the interest rate sensitivity of their deposits. Instead, the OCC encourages bank management to study the behavior of the bank's deposit accounts and develop assumptions and treatments based on how these deposits will perform under various interest rate scenarios. As important as these assumptions are in determining a bank's overall interest rate risk profile, bank management should periodically conduct sensitivity analyses on them. From these analyses, management should learn whether deposits that do not behave as assumed could hurt the bank's performance. If there is a reasonable possibility of a clearly adverse outcome, the bank should develop contingency plans. Examiners should review these analyses and plans.

Because the expected performance of these deposits will vary with a bank's competitive market, its position in that market, and its customer base, examiners should not expect every bank to treat its deposit balances the same. Examiners should determine whether the bank has analyzed its depositor base, and formulated and documented assumptions that are reasonable given the bank's past performance and its current marketing, funding, and pricing strategies.

Analyzing Nonmaturity Deposits

A bank's nonmaturity deposit base is sensitive to circumstances at the bank, in the bank's competitive market, and in the general economy. Such circumstances include:

- **The bank's need for funds and its ability to use alternative funding sources.** For example, in a period of low loan demand, a bank may change its pricing policies to allow some of its nonmaturity deposits to run off. As loan demand increases, a bank seeking to increase liquidity may raise its rates in order to attract more deposits.

- **The bank's pricing structure and customer base.** Using a variety of implicit and explicit pricing structures for its core deposits, a bank can tailor pricing for certain parts of its customer base. For example, a bank may waive certain account fees for retail customers who maintain minimum balance requirements. Commercial customers may be given an "earnings allowance" for demand deposit balances kept in lieu of paying account analysis fees. "Tiered" pricing strategies divide a bank's customer base between high-balance, rate-sensitive customers and low-balance, rate-insensitive customers. The demographics of the bank's customer base may help a bank to determine the rate sensitivity of its depositors.

- **The bank's marketing and strategic plans for its deposit products.** Many banks increasingly cluster their retail products in menus, each of which can be marketed to a segment of the customer base. In developing and planning marketing strategies, these banks may view individual products as having life cycles or market niches that influence how the bank will position and price them in the future. For example, bank management may decide to let a certain deposit product become less rate sensitive over time, and to introduce a new, more rate sensitive deposit product to customers who are more likely to move balances when interest rates change.

- **The number and type of competitors within the bank's market.** The pricing behavior of competitors will likely influence the degree and speed with which a bank will respond to changes in market interest rates. As consumers become more knowledgeable and comfortable with alternative investments, a bank's competitive market expands. Increasingly, a bank competes not only with other banks or thrifts for deposits but also with investment houses, mutual funds, and even entities that advertise their rates and services over the Internet.

- **The general level and trends of market interest rates.** Market interest rates, such as the rate that a depositor could earn by investing in Treasury securities, help to determine the "opportunity cost" to the bank's customer of maintaining bank balances. The opportunity cost of holding demand deposit balances, for example, is relatively low when market interest rates are low. As market interest rates rise, so does the opportunity cost of holding "excess" demand deposit balances. As the spread between market interest rates and the rates a bank pays on its nonmaturity deposits widens, there may be increasing incentives for bank customers to switch funds.

- **Product development and changes in financial institution regulation.** The development of new financial products and changes in banking laws can have a dramatic effect on the structure of a bank's deposit base and the behavior of depositors. For example, the elimination of regulation Q and the advent of MMDAs significantly changed the composition of a bank's deposits. When analyzing nonmaturity deposits, banks should consider any impending legislation or new products that would significantly alter the marketplace and force the bank to change its assumptions about customer behavior.

Establishing Assumptions about Nonmaturity Deposits

To determine the appropriate assumptions for its nonmaturity deposits, management should analyze carefully the bank's depositor base and the demographics of its market. Then it should assess how the circumstances described above and any other relevant factors will influence the level of deposits and the rates offered on them. Management also should consider how these factors could affect the bank's deposit base differently in alternative interest rate scenarios.

The tools bankers use to analyze deposits may vary with the size and sophistication of the bank. Larger banks will typically use tools such as regression analyses and attrition studies to help devise assumptions about deposits. The methods of smaller banks may be similar but less robust statistically.

Identifying Noncore Balances

Although bankers and regulators often refer to all the balances in a bank's DDAs, MMDAs, NOWs, and savings accounts as core balances, these accounts generally hold both core (long-term, more stable) and noncore (short-term, more temporary) balances. As a first step in analyzing its balances, bank management should isolate the amount of current balances (if any) that are "excess" or temporary balances.

Seasonal and cyclical influences cause deposit balances at many banks to fluctuate around a long-term trend line. Examples of such fluctuations may include:

- Seasonal inflows and outflows associated with business or consumer activity within the bank's market. For example, banks in resort areas or agricultural communities may have pronounced seasonal peaks and troughs in their nonmaturity deposits. Banks with sizable corporate balances may see balances temporarily increase at the end of the year or quarter. Banks serving large retirement communities may have balances that peak monthly as social security checks are deposited.

- Cyclical buildup of nonmaturity deposits. In periods of low interest rates, such increases reflect the lower "opportunity costs" that depositors incur to maintain these balances. As market interest rates rise or other investment opportunities, such as mutual funds, become more attractive, this accumulation is likely to erode as deposits shift into other products or leave the bank.

Temporary, seasonal, or cyclical inflows are often the balances that are most likely to leave the bank or move to another of the bank's funding vehicles, such as retail CDs. As a result, banks often view these balances as relatively short-term deposits. In a gap report, a bank might place these balances in a short-term (six months or less) time band. In a simulation model, a bank may forecast the departure of these balances or their shift into other products.

Estimating the Effective Maturity of Core Balances

A more difficult task when analyzing nonmaturity deposits is devising assumptions for the core balances. In developing these assumptions, bank management should consider the effect that changes in market interest rates have on the level of deposits and the rates the bank pays on them.

Interest Rate Effect

The deposit rates offered by many banks lag market interest rates and move in smaller increments than market rates do. Bank management often has deposit rates follow market rates more slowly when rates are increasing and more quickly when rates are declining. As a result, the effective maturity of the bank's deposits will tend to be longer when rates are rising and shorter when rates are falling.

Banks often place implicit caps and floors on nonmaturity deposit rates. (Some bankers and industry analysts do not acknowledge the existence of caps and floors.) A floor, which is the lowest rate a bank will pay on a deposit, reduces the implicit benefit of the deposit to the bank when interest rates are falling. A cap, which is the highest rate it will pay, raises the benefit of the deposit to the bank when interest rates are rising.

Effect on Balances

When the spread between what a bank is paying a depositor and what the depositor can earn somewhere else gets too large, the depositor will leave the bank or move to a higher-rate investment at the bank. By tracking this spread and managing the "opportunity costs" to depositors of maintaining relatively low-paying balances, bank management can influence its level of nonmaturity deposits. (Bankers often estimate opportunity costs by calculating the spread between what a customer can earn on an alternative investment outside the bank and the rate being offered by the bank.)

Past and Future

Experience should guide bank management in developing its assumptions about nonmaturity deposits. What effect has the movement of interest rates had in the past on the spread between market rates and the bank's deposit rates? What effect have changes in the spread had on the level of core deposits? Management should also be guided by the outlook for the bank. How will expected changes in the bank's competitive environment and customer base affect its pricing behavior? Persons developing assumptions should work with marketing and retail managers to get their opinions on pricing strategies.

Incorporating Assumptions into Risk Measurement

Using one method or another, banks incorporate the effect of market interest rates on deposit rates and balances into their interest rate risk measurements. Four of these methods are discussed below.

Rate Sensitive and Rate Insensitive in Gap Reports

Some banks that use gap reports stratify their nonmaturity deposits across a number of time bands. The bank's noncore or temporary balances are often reported in the shorter time bands (e.g., six months or less). The remaining balances are sometimes separated into interest sensitive and interest insensitive components.

To determine the interest sensitive portion of balances, the bank may project that it will match in deposit rates a certain percentage of market-rate movements. For example, the bank may decide that if market interest rates rise by 200 basis points, it will increase its MMDA rate by 75 basis points. This increase in its MMDA rate represents approximately 37 percent of the movement in market rates, suggesting that 37 percent of the bank's MMDA accounts are effectively rate sensitive. This portion of the bank's MMDA balances would then be reported in the shorter time bands of the bank's gap report.

Although non-interest-bearing deposits do not pay interest explicitly, a bank may determine that a portion of these balances are responsive to changes in market interest rates. For example, many corporate DDA customers maintain compensating demand balances or balances held in lieu of service charge fees. The balances are often associated with corporate cash management and account analysis services. The level of compensating balances held by corporate customers is typically driven by the earnings allowance assigned by the bank, which, in turn, often depends on market interest rates, such as the prevailing short-term CD rate. Because the level of balances will vary with this allowance rate, compensating balances are often viewed as rate sensitive in the bank's gap report.

After the bank has stratified its rate sensitive and noncore balances into shorter maturity bands, it must then determine how to treat the remaining balances in its gap report. The maturity attributed to these balances is especially important when evaluating whether the bank's nonmaturity deposits hedge the bank's economic exposure. By attributing a long maturity to these balances, bank management is assuming that the balances will not reprice or migrate to other deposit products when market interest rates change. These balances generally will be available to fund some of the bank's long-term assets.

Accordingly, the stability of the portion of nonmaturity balances that a bank considers to be rate insensitive is a critical assumption in the bank's interest rate risk measurement process. Nevertheless, banks determine maturity in many different ways. For example, a bank can:

- **View the entire remaining balance of long-term deposits as insensitive and assume that these balances effectively never reprice or mature.** Arguments provided to support such a treatment often point to the bank as an ongoing business. Under this approach the bank assumes that maturing balances (balances that become unavailable to the bank because of demographic factors such as customers moving or dying) are replaced by new customers and accounts. Sensitivity analyses should be conducted on this assumption to ensure that the bank could withstand the impact on earnings and liquidity of balances leaving the bank or migrating to other bank products.

- **Spread balances across a number of maturity bands, based on assumptions about customer attrition over time.**

- **View the remaining balances as fairly insensitive but set a maximum allowable maturity beyond which all remaining balances are assumed to run off or shift to an alternative investment.** Banks adopting this view often point to the difficulty of predicting customer behavior and industry, competitive, and regulatory conditions. These uncertainties, they suggest, warrant some limit on the maturity assumed for nonmaturity deposits.

Pricing Spreads and Balance Mix in Net Income Simulation Models

A bank developing an earnings simulation model will usually incorporate cap/floor effects and the effect of market rates on deposit rates and balances. Most simulation models will do so through the model's pricing and volume relationships. For example, the model may establish a different pricing relationship between MMDAs and rising interest rates than between MMDAs and falling rates. When rates rise 200 basis points, MMDA rates might increase by 75 basis points; when rates fall 200 basis points, MMDA rates might decrease by 125 basis points. If the bank has a lagged pricing response for its nonmaturity deposits, the speed and amount of the lag may vary with the level and direction of rates. (The lag could be larger and longer when rates are increasing.) Some banks may include an "equilibrium" reset process so that, over time, the spread between the bank's deposit rate and market rates maintains a certain stability.

To reflect the effect of market rates on deposit balances, a bank using simulation models will often lower the level of balances in a deposit category or add new balances according to the rate scenario. In the example above, because the bank's MMDA rates are expected to be less responsive in a rising rate environment, the model may lower the level of balances in the rising rate scenario.

Because the time horizon used by most earnings simulation models is two years, many banks using simulation models do not make explicit assumptions about how their nonmaturity deposits will behave over a longer period of time or for their effective maturity. However, for the reasons cited in the discussion regarding the treatment of deposits in gap reports, it is important for management to consider this issue. Implicitly, bank management is probably making some assumption about the maturity of these deposits when it is making decisions about its overall balance sheet structure and the term of investments and loans it wishes to hold.

Replicating Portfolio Analyses

Some larger banks have found it helpful to think of their nonmaturity deposit accounts as a portfolio of instruments that have different interest rate and maturity characteristics, reflecting the different pricing and strategies for account segments. To estimate the effective maturity of this portfolio of accounts, the bank performs various statistical studies on how closely a hypothetical portfolio, composed of instruments with known maturities and repricing characteristics, tracks the observed performance (e.g., level and speed of rate changes when market rates move) of the bank's deposit accounts. For example, a bank may determine that changes in a hypothetical portfolio with a mix of three-month Treasury bills and 10-year Treasury notes most closely matches the observed changes in the bank's savings rates. The bank would then use the duration or effective maturity of this hypothetical portfolio to estimate the maturity of its savings deposits.

Market Value Approach

Some banks use a market value approach to value their nonmaturity deposits. Unlike the portfolio analysis described above, the market value approach uses the duration and convexity of the deposit account cash flows themselves rather than a portfolio of instruments whose performance mirrors that of the deposits. The bank determines a market or economic value of its nonmaturity deposits by discounting the projected cash flows associated with the deposits. Models estimate the deposit cash flows for various interest rates scenarios based on the historical sensitivity of the deposits.

Interest Rate Risk

Appendix H

Funds Transfer Pricing

Some banks may centralize the management of interest rate risk in a unit of the bank, usually the treasury unit, using a funds transfer pricing system. Funds transfer pricing allows the bank to transfer the impact on earnings of changing interest rates from individual business lines to the central unit. The earnings of the business lines can then be traced more directly to the business decisions of management. Funds transfer pricing also induces line managers to make pricing decisions that are consistent with the interest rate risk management objectives of ALCO and treasury. (Banks often use funds transfer pricing to evaluate and enhance the performance of business units.)

The transfer pricing system removes interest rate risk profits and losses from individual business units. Banks can use several methods to determine the price of transferred funds. Using a "gap approach," a bank can group its assets and liabilities based on the maturity and repricing characteristics of the instruments and assign a transfer rate to each group. Alternatively, the treasury unit of a bank could assign a cost or earnings rate to every transaction. For example, treasury assigns a cost of funds to the commercial lending units for loans. A fixed rate, five-year loan might be assigned a cost-of-funds equivalent to the rate paid by the bank to borrow five-year money. The treasury will assign an earnings credit to the deposit or retail unit for the funds raised. In this way, the treasury unit acts as a middleman between the lending and retail units.

Under a transfer pricing system, profits and losses arising from interest rate mismatches are transferred to a central unit, generally the treasury department. The treasury, which is responsible for funding the loans, may either match-fund the loans or maintain the repricing mismatch. If loans are matched-funded, no interest rate risk is assumed by either the lending units or treasury. If treasury decides to maintain the mismatch, perhaps funding a five-year fixed rate loan with a one-year deposit, the unit would earn the difference between its actual funding costs and what it has charged the lending units. For example, if treasury charges the lending units 10 percent for five-year funds and raises one-year money at 9 percent, treasury would earn a 1 percent spread. Obviously, the treasury unit has assumed interest rate risk. If rates were to rise, the spread earned could decline or even become negative.

Interest Rate Risk

OCC Issuances

Capital   *Comptroller's Handbook*: "Capital and Dividends"

Derivatives   OCC Banking Circular 277

Comptroller's Handbook: "Risk Management
of Financial Derivatives"

Interagency Issuances

Interest Rate Risk   OCC Issuance 96-36

Regulations

Determination of Minimum Capital Ratios   12 CFR 3
Safety and Soundness Standards   12 CFR 30

Suggested Readings

General Interest Rate Risk

American Bankers Association, *Bank Investments & Funds Management*. Washington, DC; American Bankers Association; 1991.

Bank Administration Institute and McKinsey and Co., Inc. *Banking Off the Balance Sheet*. 1994

Gup, Benton E. and Robert Brooks. *Interest Rate Risk Management: The Banker's Guide to Using Futures, Options, Swaps and Other Derivative Instruments*. Chicago, Illinois: Bankers Publishing Co; 1993.

McGuire, William J. and Financial Managers Society. *1996 Interest Rate Risk Survey Results*. Chicago, Illinois: Financial Managers Society; 1996.

McGuire, William J. and Financial Managers Society. *Understanding and Managing Interest Rate Risk: A Director's Guide*. Chicago, Illinois: Financial Managers Society; 1994.

McGuire, William J. and Financial Managers Society. Understanding and Managing Interest Rate Risk: A Practitioner's Guide. Chicago, Illinois: Financial Managers Society; 1994.

Olson Research Associates, Inc. *Community Bank Guide to Asset/Liability Management Policies*. Washington, DC: American Bankers Association; 1991.

Basis Risk

Jackson, William E. III. "Is the Market Well Defined in Bank Merger and Acquisition Analysis?" *The Review of Economics and Statistics*, Volume LXXIV, Number 4 (November 1992), 655-661.

Jacobs, Rodney L. "The Rate Maturity of Prime and Other Indexed Assets or Liabilities." *Journal of Bank Research*, Volume 15, Number 2 (Summer 1984), 108-114.

Core Deposits

Benston, George and Mike Carhill. "The Causes and Consequences of the Thrift Disaster." *Research in Financial Services: Private and Public Policy, Volume 6*, George C. Kaufman, ed. Greenwich, Connecticut JAI Press, LTD.; 1994, 103-168.

Carhill, Mike. "Accounting Income and Market Prices: Explaining Core-Deposit Premiums." *Managerial Finance*,

Volume 23, No. 2 (1997), 42-64.

Federal Deposit Insurance Corporation, Financial Statistics and Analysis Branch, Division of Management Systems and Financial Statistics. *Regulation Q: A Historical Overview.* Financial-Statistical Report 77-4, Federal Deposit Insurance Corporation.

Flannery, Mark J. and Christopher M. James. "Market Evidence on the Effective Maturity of Bank Assets and Liabilities." *Journal of Money, Credit, and Banking,* Vol. 16, No. 4 (November 1984, Part 1), 435-445.

Hannan, Timothy H. "Asymmetric Price Rigidity and the Responsiveness of Customers to Price Changes: The Case of Deposit Interest Rates." *Journal of Financial Services Research,* Volume 8, Number 4 (December 1994), 257-267.

Hutchinson, David E. and George G. Pennacchi. "Measuring Rents and Interest Rate Risk in Imperfect Financial Markets: The Case of Retail Bank Deposits." *Journal of Financial and Quantitative Analysis,* Volume 31, Number 3 (September 1996), 399-417.

Jacklin, Charles J. "Market Rate Versus Fixed Rate Demand Deposits." *Journal of Monetary Economics,* Volume 32, No. 2 (November 1993), 237-258.

Neumark, David and Steven A. Sharpe. "Market Structure and the Nature of Price Rigidity: Evidence From the Market for Consumer Deposits." Board of Governors of the Federal Reserve System, December 1988.

O'Brien, James M., Athanasios Orphanides, and David Small. "Estimating the Interest Rate Sensitivity of Liquid Retail Deposit Values." *Proceedings of 30th Annual Conference on Bank Structure and Competition.* Chicago: Federal Reserve Bank of Chicago (May 1994), 400-435.

Selvaggio, Robert D. "Using the OAS Methodology to Value and Hedge Commercial Bank Retail Demand Deposit Premiums." *The Handbook of Asset/Liability Management,* Frank J. Fabozzi and Atsuo Konishi, ed. Irwin; 1995, 363-374.

Hedging Techniques

Brotherton-Ratcliffe, Rupert. "Monte Carlo Motoring." *Risk,* Vol. 7. No. 12 (December 1994), 52-56.

Hilliard, Jimmy E. and Susan D. Jordan. "Hedging Interest Rate Risk Under Term Structure Effects: An Application to Financial Institutions." *The Journal of Financial Research,* Vol. XV, No. 4 (Winter 1992), 355-368.

Joy, Corwin, Phelim P. Boyle, and Ken Seng Tan. "Quasi-Monte Carlo Methods in Numerical Finance." Houston, Texas: Enron Corporation (February 1995).

Selvaggio, Robert D. "An Options Approach to Valuing and Hedging Mortgage Servicing Rights." *Handbook of Fixed Income Options,* Frank J. Fabozzi, ed. Irwin, 1995.

Model Errors and Model Values

Bernard, Victor L. "Accounting-Based Valuation Methods, Determinants of Market-to-Book Ratios, and Implications for Financial Statements Analysis." Working Paper, Michigan Business School, University of Michigan (1993).

Carhill, Mike. "Information and Accuracy in Interest-Rate-Risk Simulation." OCC Economic & Policy Analysis Working Paper 94-7 (October 1994).

Eccher, Elizabeth A., K. Ramesh, and S. Ramu Thiagarajan. "Fair Value Disclosure by Bank Holding Companies." Working Paper, J.L. Kellogg Graduate School of Management, Northwestern University, Evanston Ill 60208-2002.

Irmler, Ed and Elizabeth Mays. "Maturity Gap Models Leave Balance Sheets Exposed." *Bank Accounting and Finance,* Volume 5, Number 4 (Summer 1992), 59-62.

KPMG Peat Marwick. *Estimating Fair Values for Financial Instruments: Disclosure and Beyond. A Study Prepared for the Association of Reserve City Bankers.* KPMG Peat Marwick: United States; 1993.

Schwartz, Eduardo S. and Walter N. Torous. "Caps on Adjustable Rate Mortgages: Valuation, Insurance, and Hedging." *Financial Markets and Financial Crises,* R. Glenn Hubbard, ed. Chicago: The University of Chicago Press; 1991, 283-303.

Net Interest Margin

Thistle, Paul D., Robert W. McLeod, and B. Lynne Conrad. "Interest Rates and Bank Portfolio Adjustments." *Journal of Banking and Finance*, Vol 13., No. 1 (March 1989), 151-161.

Titman, Sheridan. "Interest Rate Swaps and Corporate Financing Choices." *Journal of Finance*, Vol. XLVII, No 4 (September 1992), 1503-1516.

Zarruk, Emilio R. and Jeff Madura. "Optimal Bank Interest Margin Under Capital Regulation and Deposit Insurance." *Journal of Financial and Quantitative Analysis*, Vol. 27, No. 1 (March 1992), 143-149.

Options Pricing Issues

Cooper, Shelley and Stephanie Weston, "The Pricing of Over-the-Counter Options." *Bank of England Quarterly Bulletin*, November 1995, 375-381.

Kau, James B., Donald C. Keenan, Walter J. Muller III, and James F. Epperson. "Option Theory and Floating rate Securities with a comparison of Adjustable Rate and Fixed Rate Mortgages." *The Journal of Business*, Volume 66, Number 4 (October 1993), 595-618.

Stock Market's View of Financial Intermediaries' Interest Rate Sensitivity

Akella, Srinivas R. and Stuart I. Greenbaum. "Innovations in Interest Rates, Duration Transformation, and Bank Stock Returns." *Journal of Money, Credit, and Banking*, Vol. 24, No. 1 (February 1992), 27-42.

Choi, Jongmoo Jay, Elyas Elyasiani, and Kenneth J. Kopecky. "The Sensitivity of Bank Stock Returns to Market, Interest, and Exchange Rate Risks." *Journal of Banking and Finance*, Volume 16, No. 5 (September 1992), 983-1004.

Duan, Jin-Chuan, Arthur F. Moreau, and C.W. Sealey. "Deposit Insurance and Bank Interest-Rate Risk: Pricing and Regulatory Implications." *Journal of Banking & Finance*, Volume 19, Number 6 (September 1995), 1091-1108.

Lumpkin, Steve and James M. O'Brien. "Thrift Stock Returns and Portfolio Interest Rate Sensitivity." Board of Governors of the Federal Reserve System, October 1996.

McCulloch, J.Huston. "Measuring the Term Structure of Interest Rates," *Journal of Business*, Volume 44, Number 1 (1971), 19-31.

Term-Structure (Yield Curve) Models

Dybvig, Philip H. and William J. Marshall. "Pricing Long Bonds: Pitfalls and Opportunities." *Financial Analysts Journal*, January-February 1996, 32-39.

Ederington, Louis H. and Chao-Hsi Huang. "Parameter Uncertainty and the Rational Expectations Model of the Term Structure." *Journal of Banking and Finance*, Volume 19, Number 2 (May 1995), 207-223.

de Munnik, Jeroen F.J. and Peter C. Schotman. "Cross-Sectional versus Time Series Estimation of Term Structure Models: Empirical Results for the Dutch Bond Market." *Journal of Banking and Finance*, Volume 18, Number 5 (October 1994), 997-1025.

Overdahl, James, Barry Schachter, and Ian Lang. "The Mechanics of Zero-Coupon Yield Curve Construction." *Controlling and Managing Interest Rate Risk*, Klein, Cornyn, and Lederman, ed. Prentice Hall, 1997.